The Forerunners

Romain Rolland

ESPRIOS.COM
ESPRIOS DIGITAL PUBLISHING

THE FORERUNNERS

ROMAIN ROLLAND

THE FORERUNNERS

BY

ROMAIN ROLLAND

TRANSLATED BY

EDEN AND CEDAR PAUL

HARCOURT, BRACE AND HOWE
NEW YORK 1920

TO

THE MEMORY OF

THE MARTYRS OF THE NEW FAITH

IN THE HUMAN INTERNATIONAL.

TO

JEAN JAURÈS,

KARL LIEBKNECHT, ROSA LUXEMBURG,

KURT EISNER, GUSTAV LANDAUER,

THE VICTIMS OF BLOODTHIRSTY STUPIDITY

AND MURDEROUS FALSEHOOD,

THE LIBERATORS OF THE MEN

WHO KILLED THEM.

R. R.

August, 1919.

TABLE OF CONTENTS

INTRODUCTION

THIS book is a sequel to *Above the Battle*. It consists of a number of articles written and published in Switzerland between the end of 1915 and the beginning of 1919. As collective title for the work, I have chosen "The Forerunners," for nearly all the essays relate to the dauntless few who, the world over, amid the tempests of war and universal reaction, have been able to keep their thoughts free, their international faith inviolate. The future will reverence the names of these great harbingers, who have been flouted, reviled, threatened, found guilty, and imprisoned. I speak of such as Bertrand Russell, E. D. Morel, Maxim Gorki, G. F. Nicolai, Auguste Forel, Andreas Latzko, Henri Barbusse, Stefan Zweig, and the choice spirits of France, America, and Switzerland, who have fought for freedom.

To these essays I have prefixed an ode, "Ara Pacis," written during the first days of the war. It is an act of faith in Peace and Concord. Another act of faith will comprise the final chapter. This time it will be faith in action; the faith which, in the face of the brute force of states and of tyrannical opinion, proclaims the invincible independence of Thought.

I was half inclined to add to this collection a meditation upon *Empedocles of Agrigentum and the Reign of Hatred*.[1] But it was somewhat too long, and its inclusion would have impaired the symmetry of the volume.

In republishing the articles, I have not kept to a strictly chronological order. It appeared preferable to group them in accordance with the nature of their contents or under the guidance of artistic considerations. But at the close of each essay I have mentioned the date of original publication, and, wherever possible, the date of composition.

A few more words of explanation will help the reader to understand my general design.

Above the Battle and *The Forerunners* are no more than a part of my writings on the war, writings composed during the last five years. The volumes contain those essays only which I have published in

Switzerland. Even so, the collection is far from complete, for I have not been able to gather together all these writings. Moreover, the most important materials at my disposal, as to scope and permanent value, are a register made day by day of the letters, the confidences, the moral confessions, which I have uninterruptedly received throughout these years from the free spirits and the persecuted of all nations. Here, likewise, as soberly as possible, I have recorded my own thoughts and my own part in the struggle. Unus ex multis. The register is, as it were, a picture of the untrammelled souls of the world wrestling with the unchained forces of fanaticism, violence, and falsehood. A long time must doubtless elapse before it will be judicious to publish this record. Enough that the documents in question, of which several copies have been made, will serve in times to come as a witness of our efforts, our sufferings, our unconquerable faith.

ROMAIN ROLLAND.

PARIS, *June, 1919.*

THE FORERUNNERS

I

ARA PACIS

DE profundis clamans, out of the abyss of all the hates,
To thee, Divine Peace, will I lift up my song.

The din of the armies shall not drown it.
Imperturbable, I behold the rising flood incarnadine,
Which bears the beauteous body of mutilated Europe,
And I hear the raging wind which stirs the souls of men.

Though I stand alone, I shall be faithful to thee.
I shall not take my place at the sacrilegious communion of blood.
I shall not eat my share of the Son of Man.

I am brother to all, and I love you all,
Men, ephemerals who rob yourselves of your one brief day.

Above the laurels of glory and above the oaks,
May there spring from my heart upon the Holy Mount,
The olive tree, with the sunlight in its boughs, where the cicadas sing.

*
* *

Sublime Peace who holdest,
Beneath thy sovran sway,
The turmoil of the world,
And who, from out the hurtling of the waves,
Makest the rhythm of the seas;

Cathedral established
Upon the perfect balance of opposing forces;
Dazzling rose-window,
Where the blood of the sun
Gushes forth in diapered sheaves of flame

Which the harmonising eye of the artist has bound together;

Like to a huge bird
Which soars in the zenith,
Sheltering the plain beneath its wings,
Thy flight embraces,
Beyond what is, that which has been and will be.

Thou art sister to joy and sister to sorrow,
Youngest and wisest of sisters;
Thou holdest them both by the hand.
Thus art thou like a limpid channel linking two rivers,
A channel wherein the skies are mirrored betwixt two rows of pale poplars.

Thou art the divine messenger,
Passing to and fro like the swallow
From bank to bank,
Uniting them.
To some saying,
"Weep not, joy will come again";
To others,
"Be not over-confident, happiness is fleeting."

Thy shapely arms tenderly enfold
Thy froward children,
And thou smilest, gazing on them
As they bite thy swelling breast.

Thou joinest the hands and the hearts
Of those who, while seeking one another, flee one another;
And thou subjectest to the yoke the unruly bulls,
So that instead of wasting
In fights the passion which makes their flanks to smoke,
Thou turnest this passion to account for ploughing in the womb of the land
The furrow long and deep where the seed will germinate.

Thou art the faithful helpmate
Who welcomest the weary wrestlers on their return.
Victors or vanquished, they have an equal share of thy love.
For the prize of battle
Is not a strip of land
Which one day the fat of the victor
Will nourish, mingled with that of his foe.
The prize is, to have been the tool of Destiny,
And not to have bent in her hand.

O my Peace who smilest, thy soft eyes filled with tears,
Summer rainbow, sunny evening,
Who, with thy golden fingers,
Fondlest the besprinkled fields,
Carest for the fallen fruits,
And healest the wounds
Of the trees which the wind and the hail have bruised;

Shed on us thy healing balm, and lull our sorrows to sleep!
They will pass, and we also.
Thou alone endurest for ever.

Brothers, let us unite; and you, too, forces within me,
Which clash one upon another in my riven heart!
Join hands and dance along!

We move forward calmly and without haste,
For Time is not our quarry.
Time is on our side.
With the osiers of the ages my Peace weaves her nest.

*
* *

I am like the cricket who chirps in the fields.
A storm bursts, rain falls in torrents, drowning
The furrows and the chirping.
But as soon as the flurry is over,
The little musician, undaunted, resumes his song.

In like manner, having heard, in the smoking east, on the devastated earth,
The thunderous charge of the Four Horsemen,
Whose gallop rings still from the distance,
I uplift my head and resume my song,
Puny, but obstinate.

Written August 15 to 25, 1914.[2]

"Journal de Genève" and "Neue Zürcher Zeitung," December 24 and 25, 1915; "Les Tablettes," Geneva, July, 1917.

II

UPWARDS, ALONG A WINDING ROAD

IF I have kept silence for a year, it is not because the faith to which I gave expression in *Above the Battle* has been shaken (it stands firmer than ever); but I am well assured that it is useless to speak to him who will not hearken. Facts alone will speak, with tragical insistence; facts alone will be able to penetrate the thick wall of obstinacy, pride, and falsehood with which men have surrounded their minds because they do not wish to see the light.

But we, as between brothers of all the nations; as between those who have known how to defend their moral freedom, their reason, and their faith in human solidarity; as between minds which continue to hope amid silence, oppression, and grief—we do well to exchange, as this year draws to a close, words of affection and solace. We must convince one another that during the blood-drenched night the light is still burning, that it never has been and never will be extinguished.

In the abyss of suffering into which Europe is plunged, those who wield the pen must be careful never to add an additional pang to the mass of pangs already endured, and never to pour new reasons for hatred into the burning flood of hate. Two ways remain open for those rare free spirits which, athwart the mountain of crimes and follies, are endeavouring to break a trail for others, to find for themselves an egress. Some are courageously attempting in their respective lands to make their fellow-countrymen aware of their own faults. This is the course adopted by the valiant Englishmen of the Independent Labour Party and of the Union of Democratic Control, and by those fine men of untrammelled mind Bertrand Russell, E. D. Morel, Norman Angell, Bernard Shaw; this is the path taken by certain persecuted Germans, too few in number; this is the path taken by the Italian socialists, by the Russian socialists, by Gorki, the master of Sorrow and of Pity; and this is the path taken by certain free Frenchmen.

My own task is different, for it is to remind the hostile brethren of Europe, not of their worst aspects but of their best, to recall to them reasons for hoping that there will one day be a wiser and more loving humanity.

What we now have to contemplate may, indeed, well incline us to despair of human reason. For those, and they were many, who were blissfully slumbering upon their faith in progress, a progress from which there was to be no looking back, the awakening has been rude. Without transition, such persons have passed from the absurd excesses of slothful optimism to the vertigo of unplumbed pessimism. They are not used to looking at life except from behind a parapet. A barrier of comfortable illusions has hidden from them, hitherto, the chasm above which, clinging to the face of the precipice, winds the narrow path along which man is marching. Here and there the wall has crumbled. The footing is treacherous. But we must pass, nevertheless. We shall pass. Our fathers had to make their way across many such places. We have been too ready to forget. Save for a few shocks, the years of our own lives have been spent in a sheltered age. But in the past, epochs of disturbance have been commoner than epochs of calm. What is taking place to-day is horribly abnormal for those alone who were drowsing in the abnormal peace of a society equally devoid of foresight and of remembrance. Let us call to mind those whom the past has known. Let us think of Buddha, the liberator; of the Orphics worshipping Dionysos-Zagreus, god of the innocent who suffer and will be avenged; of Xenophanes of Elea who had to witness the devastation of his fatherland by Cyrus; of Zeno tortured; of Socrates put to death by poison; of Plato dreaming during the rule of the Thirty Tyrants; of

Marcus Aurelius, sustaining the empire whose decline was at hand. Let us think of those who watched the ruin of the old world; of the bishop of Hippo dying when his city was about to fall before the onslaught of the Vandals; of the monks who, in a Europe peopled with wolves, worked as illuminators, builders, musicians. Let us think of Dante, Copernicus, and Savonarola; of exiles, persecutions, burnings at the stake; of Spinoza, frail in health, writing his immortal *Ethics* by the light of the burning villages of his invaded country. Let us think of our own Michel de Montaigne, in his defenceless castle, softly pillowed, waking from his light sleep to hear the bells pealing from the church towers of the countryside, or asking himself in his dreams if he was to be murdered that very night.... Man is not fond of reviving the memory of disagreeable occurrences; he dislikes to think of things which disturb his tranquillity. But in the history of the world, tranquillity has been rare; nor is it in a tranquil environment that the greatest souls have been fashioned. Let us without a shudder contemplate the raging flood as it passes. For those whose ears are attuned to the rhythm of history, all contributes to the same work, evil no less than good. Those of impulsive temperament, carried away by the flood, move along blood-stained roads, and are none the less moving, willy-nilly, whither fraternal reason beckons. Were we compelled to depend upon men's common sense, upon their goodwill, upon their moral courage, upon their kindliness, there would be ample reason for despairing of the future. But those who will not or cannot march, pushed onward by blind forces, a bleating flock, move towards the goal: Unity.

*

* *

The unity of our own France was forged by agelong struggles between the separate provinces. At one time every province, even every village, was a fatherland. For more than a hundred years the Armagnacs and the Burgundians (my ancestors) went on breaking one another's heads, to discover in the end that they were men of one blood. The war which is now mingling the blood of France and of Germany, is leading the French and the Germans to drink from the same cup to their future union, like the barbaric heroes of the epic age. Struggle and bite as they may, their very grapple binds them together. These armies which are endeavouring to destroy one another, have become more akin in spirit than they were before they faced one another in battle. They can kill one another, but at least they now know one another, whereas ignorance is the nethermost circle of death. Numerous testimonies from the opposing fronts have borne clear witness to the mutual desire of the soldiers, though still fighting, to understand one another. Men who from trench to enemy trench watch one another while taking aim, may remain foes, but they are no longer strangers. At no distant day a union of the nations of the west will form a new fatherland, which itself will be but a stage upon the road leading to a still greater fatherland, that of Europe. Do we not already see the dozen states of Europe, divided into two camps, unwittingly attempting to build a federation wherein war between nations will be no less sacrilegious than would now be war between provinces; a federation in which the duty of to-day will be the crime of to-morrow? Has not the need for this future union been affirmed by the most conflicting voices: by William II, who spoke of the "United States of Europe";[3] by Hanotaux, with his "European Confederation";[4] by Ostwald, and Haeckel of lamentable memory, with their "Society of States"? Each one, doubtless, worked for his own saint; but all these saints served the same master!...

Nay more, the gigantic chaos wherein, as if amid the throes that occurred when the earth was still molten, all the human elements from the three continents of the Old World are clashing one against another, is a racial alchemy preparing, alike by force and by spiritual factors, alike by war and by peace, the coming fusion of the two halves of the world, of the two hemispheres of thought, of Europe and Asia. I do not talk utopia. For some years this drawing together has been preluded by a thousand signs, by mutual attraction in the realms of thought and of art, in the realms of politics and of commerce. The war has merely accelerated the movement; and while the war yet rages, men are at work on behalf of this cause. Two years ago, in one of the belligerent states, there were founded great institutes for the comparative study of the civilisations of Europe and of Asia, and to promote their mutual penetration.

"The most striking phenomenon of our day," thus runs the program of one of these institutes,[5] "is the formation of a universal civilisation, issuing from a number of distinct civilisations handed down from earlier days.... No past epoch has ever beheld a more powerful impetus animating the human race than that which mankind has known during recent centuries and the one we have now entered. There has been nothing comparable to this torrential confluence of all the forces to form a resultant, the achievement of the nineteenth and twentieth centuries. In the state, in science, and in art, everywhere, there is now being elaborated the great individuality of universal mankind; everywhere there is uprising the new life of the universal human spirit.... The three spiritual and social worlds, the three mankinds (that of Europe and the Near East, that of Hindustan, and that of the Far East) are beginning to be assembled to form a single mankind.... Until two generations ago, the individual man was member of a single branch of mankind, of one distinct great form of life. Now he participates in a vast vital flux constituted by the whole of mankind; he must direct his actions in accordance with the laws of that flux, and must find his own place in it. Should he fail to do this, he will lose the best part of himself.—Doubtless, the most significant features of the past, of its religions, of its art, of its thought, are not in question. These remain, and will remain. But they will be raised to new altitudes, dug to new depths. A wider circle of life is opening around us. We need not be surprised that many become giddy and imagine that the greatness of the past is decaying. But the helm must be entrusted to those who are competent, calmly and firmly, to make things ready for the new age.... The completest happiness which can accrue to man henceforward, will be derived from the intelligence of mankind as a whole, and from the multiple ways which man has discovered of attaining happiness.... For a long time to come the intensest joy which man can know on earth will derive from supplementing the ideals of Europe by the ideals of Asia."

Researches of this nature, characterised by universality and objectivity, "formally exclude," continues the program, "everything that tends to foster hatred among nations, classes, and races; everything that induces disintegration and useless struggle.... Those who are engaged in such researches have to fight one thing above all, to fight hatred, ignorance, and lack of understanding.... Their splendid and urgent task is to bring to light the beauty which exists in every human individuality and every nation; their task is the practical one of discovering the scientific means of adjusting differences between nations, classes, and races. Science, and science alone, is competent, by strenuous labour, to win peace...."

Thus amid the warfare of the nations are being laid the foundations of spiritual peace between the nations, like a lighthouse which reveals to widely separated vessels the distant haven where they will anchor side by side. The human mind has reached the gateway leading into a new road. The gateway is too narrow, and people are crushing one another as they endeavour to get through. But beyond it I see stretching the broad highway along which they will move and where there is room for all. Amid the encircling horrors, the vision comforts me. My heart suffers, but my spirit sees the light.

*

* *

Take courage, brothers! Despite all, there are good reasons for hope. Willy-nilly, men are advancing towards our goal; even those who think they have turned their backs on it. In 1887, when the ideas of democracy and international peace bade fair to triumph, I was talking to Renan, who uttered these prophetic words: "You will live to see another great reaction. It may seem to you then that all we are defending has been destroyed. But rest easy in your mind. Humanity's road is a mountain path, winding to and fro among the spurs, so that at times we fancy that we are going away from the summit. But we never cease to climb."

Everything is working on behalf of our ideal; even those are working for it whose blows are directed towards its ruin. Everything makes for unity, the worst no less than the best. Let no one interpret me as implying that the worst is as good as the best! Between the misguided ones who (poor innocents!) preach the war that will end war (those whom we may name the "bellipacifists"), and the unqualified pacifists, those who take their stand upon the gospels, there is a difference like that between madmen who, desiring to get quickly from the attic into the street, would throw furniture and children out of the window—and those who walk down the stairs. Progress is achieved; but nature does not hurry, and her methods are wasteful. The most trifling advance is secured by a terrible squandering of wealth and of lives.[6] When Europe, moving reluctantly, haltingly, like a sorry screw, comes at length to the conviction that she must unify her forces, the union, alas, will be a union of the blind and the paralytic. She will reach the goal, but will be bloodless and exhausted.

For our part, however, we have long been awaiting you there; long ago we achieved unity, we, the free spirits of all the ages, all the classes, and all the races. Those belonging to the remote civilisations of Egypt and the east; the Socrates' and the Lucians of the modern age, such as Thomas More, Erasmus, and Voltaire; those belonging to a distant future, a future which will perchance (looping the loop of time) return to the thought of Asia—the great and the simple, but all free spirits and all brothers, we are but one people. The centuries of the persecutions, the wide world round, have linked us heart and hand. It is this unbreakable chain, encompassing the clay image we term civilisation, which keeps the frail structure from falling to pieces.

"Le Carmel," Geneva, December, 1916.

III

TO THE MURDERED PEOPLES

THE horrors that have taken place during the last two and a half years have given a rude spiritual shock to the western world. No one can ever forget the martyrdom of Belgium, Serbia, Poland, of all the unhappy lands of the west and of the east trampled by invaders. Yet these iniquitous deeds, by which we are revolted because we ourselves are the sufferers—for half a century or more, European civilisation has been doing them or allowing them to be done.

Who will ever know at what a price the Red Sultan has purchased from his mutes of the European press and European diplomacy their silence concerning the slaughter of two hundred thousand Armenians during the first massacres, those of 1894 to 1896? Who will voice the sufferings of the peoples delivered over to rapine during colonial enterprises? When a corner of the veil has been lifted, when in Damaraland or the Congo we have been given a glimpse of one of these fields of pain, who has been able to bear the sight without a shudder? What "civilised" man can think without a blush of the massacres of Manchuria and of the expedition to China in 1900 and 1901, when the German emperor held up Attila as an example to his soldiers, when the allied armies of the "civilised world" rivalled one another in acts of vandalism against a civilisation older and nobler than that of the west?[7] What help has the western world given to the persecuted races of eastern Europe, to the Jews, the Poles, the Finns, etc.?[8] What aid to Turkey and to China in their efforts towards regeneration? Sixty years ago, China, poisoned by Indian opium, wished to free herself from the deadly vice. But after two wars and a humiliating peace, she had to accept from England this poison, which is said during a century to have brought to the East India Company profits amounting to £440,000,000. Even in our own day, when China, by a heroic effort, had within ten years cured herself of this disastrous sickness, the sustained pressure of public opinion was requisite to compel the most highly civilised of the European states to renounce the profits derived from the poisoning of a nation. The facts need hardly surprise us, seeing that this same western state continues to draw revenues from the poisoning of its own subjects.

"On the Gold Coast," writes M. Arnold Porret, "a missionary once told me how the negroes account for the European's white skin. God Almighty asked him, 'What hast thou done with thy brother?' And he turned white with fear."[9]

European civilisation stinks of the dead-house. "Jam foetet...." Europe has called in the grave-diggers. Asia is on the watch.

On June 18, 1916, at the Imperial University of Tokyo, Rabindranath Tagore, the great Hindu, spoke as follows: "The political civilisation which has sprung from the soil of Europe and is overrunning the whole world, like some prolific weed, is based upon exclusiveness. It is always watchful to keep the aliens at bay or to exterminate them. It is carnivorous and cannibalistic in its tendencies, it feeds upon the resources of other peoples and tries to swallow their whole future. It is always afraid of other races achieving eminence, naming it as a peril, and tries to thwart all symptoms of greatness outside its own boundaries, forcing down races of men who are weaker, to be eternally fixed in their weakness.... This political civilisation is scientific, not human. It is powerful because it concentrates all its forces upon one purpose, like a millionaire acquiring money at the cost of his soul. It betrays its trust, it weaves its meshes of lies without shame, it enshrines gigantic idols of greed in its temples, taking great pride in the costly ceremonials of its worship, calling this patriotism. And it can safely be prophesied that this cannot go on...."[10]

"This cannot go on." Do you hear, Europeans? Are you stopping your ears? Listen to the voice within! We ourselves must question ourselves. Let us not resemble those who ascribe to their neighbour all the sins of the world, and think themselves blameless. For the curse under which we are labouring to-day, each one of us must bear his share of responsibility. Some have erred by deliberate choice, others through weakness, and it is not the weak who are the least guilty. The apathy of the majority, the timorousness of the well-meaning, the selfishness and scepticism of listless rulers, the ignorance or cynicism of the press, the rapacity of profiteers, the faint-hearted servility of the thinkers who make themselves the apostles of devastating prejudices which it should be their mission to uproot; the ruthless pride of intellectuals who value their own ideas more than they value the lives of their fellow-men, and who will send millions to death to prove themselves in the right; the counsels of expediency of a church that is too Roman, a church in which St. Peter the fisherman has become the ferryman of diplomacy; pastors with arid souls, with souls keen-edged as a knife, immolating their flocks in the hope of purifying them; the blind submission of the silly sheep.... Who among us is free from blame? Who among us can wash his hands of the blood of a butchered Europe? Let each one admit his fault and endeavour to expiate it!—But let us turn to the most immediate task.

Here is the outstanding fact: EUROPE IS NOT FREE. The voice of the nations is stifled. In the history of the world, these years will be looked upon as the years of the great Slavery. One half of Europe is fighting the other half, in the name of liberty. That they may fight the better, both halves of Europe have renounced liberty. An appeal to the will of the nations is fruitless. As individual entities, THE NATIONS NO LONGER EXIST. A handful of politicians, a few score journalists, have the audacity to speak in the name of this nation or of that. They have no right to speak. They represent no one but themselves. They do not even represent themselves. As early as 1905, Maurras, denouncing the tamed intelligentsia which claims to lead opinion and to represent the nation, spoke of it as "ancilla plutocratiae." ... The nation! Who has the right to call himself the representative of a nation? Who knows the soul, who has ever dared to look into the soul, of a nation at war? It is a monster, composed of many myriads of conglomerated lives, of lives that are distinct and conflicting, lives that move in all directions and are yet joined at the base like the tentacles of an octopus.... It is a confused mingling of all the instincts, and of all the reasons, and of all the unreasons.... Blasts of wind from the abyss; sightless and raging forces issuing from the seething depths of animalism; a mad impulse towards destruction and self-destruction; the crude appetites of the herd; distorted religion; mystical erections of the soul enamoured of the infinite, and seeking the morbid assuagement of joy through suffering, through its own suffering, and through the suffering of others; the pretentious despotism of reason, claiming the right to impose on others the unity it lacks yet desires; romanticist flashes of an imagination kindled by memories of the past; the academic phantasmagoria of official history, of the patriotic history which is ever ready to brandish the "Vae Victis" of Brennus, or the "Gloria Victis," as circumstances may dictate.... Helter-skelter there surge upon the tide of passion all the lurking fiends which, in times of peace and order, society spurns.... Every one of us is entangled in the tentacles of the octopus. Every one of us discovers in himself the same confusion of good and of bad impulses, knotted and intertwined. A tangled skein. Who shall unravel it?... Thence comes the feeling of inexorable fate by which, in such crises, men are overwhelmed. Nevertheless this feeling derives merely from their own despondency in face of the efforts necessary to free themselves, efforts manifold and prolonged, but within the compass of their powers. If each one did what he could (no more would be required!) fate would not prove inexorable. The apparent fatality results from the universal abdication. By abandoning himself to fate, each one incurs a share of the guilt.

But the shares in the guilt are unequal. Honour to whom honour is due! In the loathsome stew which European politics constitute to-day, money is the tit-bit. Society is enchained, and the hand holding the chain is the hand of Plutus. He is the real master, the real ruler, of the states. It is he who makes of them fraudulent firms, swindling enterprises.[11] The reader must not suppose that we wish to fix the whole responsibility for the ills we are now enduring upon this or that social group, upon this or that individual. We are not such innocents; we have no wish to make a scapegoat of anyone! This would be too easy a solution. We shall not even say, "Is fecit cui prodest." We shall not say that those desired the war who are now shamelessly profiting by the war. All that they want is profit, and how the profit is made is of no moment to them. They accommodate themselves equally well to war and to peace, to peace and to war, for all is grist which comes to their mill. Let us give one example among a thousand to show how indifferent these men of money become to everything but money. It is a matter of recent history that a group of great German capitalists bought mines in Normandy and gained possession of a fifth part of the mineral wealth of France. Between 1908 and 1913, developing for their own profit the iron industry of our country, they helped in the production of the cannons whose fire is now sweeping the German lines. Such a man was the fabled Midas of antiquity, King Midas of the golden touch.... Do not suppose them to entertain hidden but far-reaching designs. They are men of short views. Their aim is to pile up as much wealth as they can, as quickly as possible. In them we see the climax of that anti-social egoism which is the curse of our day. They are merely the most typical figures in an epoch enslaved to money. The intellectuals, the press, the politicians, the very members of the cabinets (preposterous puppets!), have, whether they like it or not, become tools in the hands of the profiteers, and act as screens to hide them from the public eye.[12] Meanwhile the stupidity of the peoples, their fatalistic submissiveness, the mysticism they have inherited from their primitive ancestors, leave them defenceless before the hurricane of lying and frenzy which drives them to mutual slaughter....

There is a wicked and cruel saying that nations always have the governments they deserve. Were this true, we should have reason to despair of mankind, for where can we find a government with which a decent man would shake hands? It is all too clear that the masses, those who work, are unable to exercise due control over the men who rule them. Enough for the masses that they invariably have to pay for the errors or the crimes of their rulers. It would be too much, in addition, to make those who are ruled responsible. The men of the people, sacrificing themselves, die for ideas. Those who send others to the sacrifice, live for interests. Thus it comes to pass that the interests live longer than the ideas. Every prolonged war, even a war which at the outset was in a high degree idealistic, tends more and more, as it is protracted, to become a business matter, to become, as Flaubert wrote, "a war for money."—Let me repeat, there is no suggestion that the war is undertaken for money. But as soon as the war is afoot, the milking begins; blood flows, money flows, and no one is in a hurry to stop the flow. A few thousands of privileged persons, belonging to all castes and all nations, a few thousands, men of family, parvenus, junkers, ironmasters, syndicated speculators, army contractors, untitled and irresponsible kings—hidden in the wings, surrounded by and nourishing a swarm of parasites—are able, for the sordid motive of gain, to turn to their own account the best and the worst instincts of mankind. They profit by human ambition and by human pride; by men's grudges and men's hates. They draw equal gains from the bloodthirsty imaginings and from the courage of their fellow-mortals; from the thirst for self-sacrifice, from the heroism which makes men eager to spill their own blood, from the inexhaustible wealth of faith!...

Unhappy peoples! Is it possible to imagine a more tragical destiny than theirs? Never consulted, always immolated, thrust into war, forced into crimes which they have never wished to commit. Any chance adventurer or braggart arrogantly claims the right to cloak with the name of the people the follies of his murderous rhetoric or the sordid interests he wishes to satisfy. The masses are everlastingly duped, everlastingly martyred; they pay for others' misdeeds. Above their heads are exchanged challenges for causes of which they know nothing and for stakes which are of no interest to them. Across their backs, bleeding and bowed, takes place the struggle of ideas and of millions, while they themselves have no more share in the former than in the latter. For their part, they do not hate. They are the sacrifice; and those only hate who have ordered the sacrifice. Peoples poisoned by lies, by the press, by alcohol, and by harlots. Toiling masses, who must now unlearn the lesson of labour. Generous-hearted masses, who must now unlearn the lesson of brotherly love. Masses deliberately demoralised, given over to corruption while still alive, slain. Beloved peoples of Europe, dying for the last two years on your dying land. Have you at length plumbed the depths of woe? Alas, the worst is yet to come. After so much anguish, I dread the fatal day when, no longer buoyed by false hopes, realising the fruitlessness of their sacrifices, the masses, worn out with misery, will blindly wreak their vengeance where they may. They, likewise, will then fall into injustice, and through a surfeit of misfortune they will forfeit even the sombre halo of self-sacrifice. Then, from one end of the chain to the other, all alike will be plunged in the same sea of pain and error. Poor crucified wretches, struggling on your crosses on either side of the Master's! Betrayed more cruelly than He, instead of floating, you will sink like a stone in the ocean of your agony. Will no one save you from your two foes, slavery and hatred? We wish to, we wish to! But you, too, must wish it. Do you wish it? For centuries your reason has been bridled in passive obedience. Are you still capable of achieving freedom?

Who is able to-day to stop the war in its progress? Who can recapture the wild beast and put it back into its cage? Perhaps not even those who first loosed it, the beast-tamers who know that soon will come their turn to be devoured. The cup has been filled with blood and must be drained to the last drop. Carouse, Civilisation! — But when thou art glutted, when peace has come again across ten million corpses and thou hast slept off thy drunken debauch, wilt thou be able to regain mastery of thyself? Wilt thou dare to contemplate thy own wretchedness stripped of the lies with which thou hast veiled it? Will that which can and must go on living, have the courage to free itself from the deadly embrace of rotten institutions?... Peoples, unite! Peoples of all races, more blameworthy or less, all bleeding and all suffering, brothers in misfortune, be brothers in forgiveness and in rebirth. Forget your rancours, which are leading you to a common doom. Join in your mourning, for the losses affect the whole great family of mankind. Through the pain, through the deaths, of millions of your brethren, you must have been made aware of your intimate oneness. See to it that after the war this unity breaks down the barriers which the shamelessness of a few selfish interests would fain rebuild more solidly than ever.

If you fail to take this course, if the war should not bring as its first fruit a social renascence in all the nations, then farewell Europe, queen of thought, guide of mankind. You have lost your way; you are marking time in a cemetery. The cemetery is the right place for you. Make your bed there. Let others lead the world!

ALL SOULS' DAY, 1916.
"demain," Geneva, November and December, 1916.

IV

TO THE UNDYING ANTIGONE

THE most potent action within the competence of us all, men and women alike, is individual action, the action of man on man, of soul on soul, action by word, by example, by the whole personality. Women of Europe, you fail to use this power as you should. You are now attempting to extirpate the plague which afflicts the world, to wage war against the war. You do well, but your action comes too late. You could have fought, you ought to have fought, against this war before it broke out; to have fought it in the hearts of men. You do not realise your power over us. Mothers, sisters, helpmates, friends, sweethearts, you are able, and you will, to mould man's soul. The soul of the child is in your hands; and in relation to a woman whom he respects and loves, a man is ever a child. Why do you not guide his footsteps? If I may give a personal example, let me say that to certain among you I owe what is best or what is least bad in my own nature. If, during this whirlwind, I have been able to maintain unshaken my faith in human brotherhood, my love of love, and my scorn of hate, I owe this to a few women. To name but two among them: I owe it to my mother, a true Christian, who in early childhood inspired me with a passion for the eternal; and I owe it to the great European, Malvida von Meysenbug, the sublime idealist, who in her serene old age was the friend of my youth. If a woman can save one man's soul, why do not you women save all men's souls? The reason, doubtless, is that too few among you have as yet saved your own souls. Begin at the beginning! Here is a matter more urgent than the conquest of political rights (whose practical importance I am far from under-rating). The most urgent matter is the conquest of yourselves. Cease to be man's shadow; cease to be the shadow of man's passions, of his pride and of his impulse towards destruction. Gain a clear vision of the brotherly duty of sympathy, of mutual aid, of the community of all beings; these make up the supreme law prescribed to Christians by the voice of Christ, and to free spirits by the free reason. Yet how many of you in Europe to-day are carried away by the gusts of passion which have overpowered the minds of men; how many of you, instead of enlightening men, add their own fever to the universal delirium!

Begin by making peace within yourselves. Rid yourselves of the spirit of blind combativeness. Do not allow yourselves to be embroiled in the struggle. You will not make an end of the war by making war on the war; your first step should be to save your own hearts from the war, by saving from the general conflagration the FUTURE WHICH IS WITHIN YOU. To each word of hatred uttered by the combatants, make answer by an act of kindness and love toward all the victims. Let your simple presence show a calm disavowal of errant passions; make of yourselves onlookers whose luminous and compassionate gaze compels us to blush at our own unreason. Amid war, be the living embodiment of peace. Be the undying Antigone, who renounces hatred, and who makes no distinction between her suffering and warring brethren.

"Jus Suffragii," London, May, 1915; "demain," Geneva, January, 1916.

V

A WOMAN'S VOICE FROM OUT THE TUMULT[13]

A WOMAN with compassion and who dares to avow it; *a woman who dares to avow her horror of war, her pity for the victims, for all the victims;* a woman who refuses to add her voice to the chorus of murderous passions; a woman genuinely French who does not endeavour to ape the heroines of Corneille. What a solace!

I wish to avoid saying anything which could hurt wounded souls. I know how much grief, how much suppressed tenderness, are hidden, in thousands of women, beneath the armour of a dogged enthusiasm. They stiffen their sinews for fear of falling. They walk, they talk, they laugh, with an open wound in the side through which the heart's blood is gushing. *No prophetic faculty is needed to foresee that the time is at hand when they will throw off this inhuman constraint, and when the world, surfeited with bloody heroism, will not hesitate to proclaim its disgust and its execration.*

From childhood onwards our minds are distorted by a state education which instills into us a rhetorical ideal, a compost of fragments torn from the vast field of classical thought, revivified by the genius of Corneille and the glories of the revolution. It is an ideal which exultantly sacrifices the individual to the state, *which sacrifices common sense to crazy ideas.* For the minds of those who have undergone this discipline, life becomes a pretentious and cruel syllogism, whose premises are obscure but whose conclusion is remorseless. Every one of us, in his time, has been subjected to its sway. No one has better reason to know than myself how terrible a struggle is required to free the spirit from this second nature which tends to stifle the first. The history of these struggles is the history of our contradictions. God be thanked, this war—nay, it is more than a war, this convulsion of mankind—will clear away our doubts, put an end to our hesitations, compel us to choose.

Marcelle Capy has chosen. The strength of her book is to be found in this, that through her *Woman's Voice from out the Tumult* there breathes the common sense of the French people, which has shaken off the sophisms of ideology and rhetoric. This free vision, living, thrilling, never deceived, is sensitive to every hint of suffering or ridicule. For in the sightless epic which racks the nations of Europe, every type of experience abounds: great exploits and great crimes, sublime acts of devotion and sordid interests, heroes and grotesques. If to laugh be permissible, if it be French to laugh amid the worst trials, how much more justifiable is laughter when it becomes a weapon against hypocrisy, a weapon employed for the vindication of stifled common sense! Never was hypocrisy more widespread and more disastrous than in these days, when in every land it is a mask assumed by force. Hypocrisy, it has been said, is the homage vice pays to virtue. Well and good; but the homage is excessive. Charming comedy, in which instincts, interests, and private revenges take shelter beneath the sacred cloak of patriotism. These Tartufes of heroism, prepared to offer up a splendid holocaust—of others! These poor Orgons, duped and sacrificed, eager to destroy those who would defend them and who seek to enlighten them! What a spectacle for a Molière or a Ben Jonson. Marcelle Capy's book presents us with a fecund collection of these perennial types which teem in our epoch, much as poisonous toadstools of unclassified species teem on rotting wood. Yet the old stumps on which they batten throw out green shoots. We perceive that the heart of the French forest is still sound; that the poison has not eaten into our vitals.[14]

Take courage, good friends, all who love France. Rest assured that the best way of doing honour to France is to maintain her reputation for good sense, geniality, and humour. Let the voice of Marcelle Capy's book, tender and valiant, be an example and a guide. Use your eyes, let your heart speak. Be not fooled by big words. *Peoples of Europe, throw off this herd mentality, the mentality of sheep who would ask the shepherds and the sheep-dogs to tell them where to feed.* Take heart! Not all the furies in the universe shall prevent the world from hearing the cry of faith and hope uttered by a single free spirit, from hearing the song of the Gallic lark winging its way heavenward!

March 21, 1916.

VI

FREEDOM

THE war has shown us how fragile are the treasures of our civilisation. Of all our goods, freedom, on which we prided ourselves most, has proved the frailest. It had been won by degrees through centuries of sacrifice, of patient effort, of suffering, of heroism, and of stubborn faith; we inhaled its golden atmosphere; our enjoyment of it seemed as natural as our enjoyment of the fresh air which sweeps across the surface of the earth and floods our lungs. A few days were enough to steal from us this jewel of life; within a few hours, the world over, the quivering wings of liberty were enmeshed as in a net. The peoples had delivered her up. Nay more, they hailed their own enslavement with acclamations. We have relearned the old truth. "No conquest is ever achieved once for all. Conquest is a continued action which must be sustained day by day under penalty of forfeiture."

Betrayed liberty, take sanctuary in the hearts of the faithful, fold your wounded pinions! In days to come you will resume your splendid flight. Then you will again be the idol of the multitude. Those who now oppress you, will then sing your praises. But in my eyes never have you seemed more beautiful than in this time of trial, when you are poor, despoiled, and stricken. You have nothing left to offer those who love you, nothing but danger and the smile of your undaunted eyes. Nevertheless, not all the wealth of the world can be compared with this gift. The lackeys of public opinion, the worshippers of success, will never compete with us for it. But we shall be true to you, Christ despised and rejected, for we know that you will rise again from the tomb.

"Avanti," Milan, May 1, 1916.

VII

FREE RUSSIA, THE LIBERATOR!

RUSSIAN brothers, who have just achieved your great revolution, we have not merely to congratulate you; we have in addition to thank you. In your conquest of freedom, you have not been working for yourselves alone, but for us likewise, for your brothers of the old west.

Human progress has been a secular evolution. Quickly getting out of breath, flagging again and again, progress slackens, jibs at obstacles, or lies down in the road like a lazy mule. To bring about a fresh start, to ensure movement from stage to stage, there must be renewed awakenings of energy, vigorous revolutionary outbursts, which stimulate the will, brace the muscles, and blow the obstacle to smithereens. Our revolution of 1789 was one of these outbursts of heroic energy, dragging mankind out of the rut wherein it had become wedged, and compelling a fresh start. But as soon as the effort has been made and the chariot set in motion, mankind has been only too ready to stick fast in the mire again. Long ago, the French revolution brought all that it could bring to Europe. A time comes when ideas which were once fertilising, ideas which were once the forces of renewed life, are no longer anything more than idols of the past, forces tending to drag us backwards, additional obstacles. Such has been the lesson of the world war, in which the jacobins of the west have often proved the worst enemies of liberty.

For new times, new paths and new aspirations! Russian brothers, your revolution has come to awaken this Europe of ours, drowsing over the arrogant memories of whilom revolutions. March onward! We will follow in your footsteps. The nations take it in turn to lead humanity. It is for you, whose youthful vitality has been hoarded during centuries of enforced inactivity, to pick up the axe where we have let it fall. In the virgin forest of social injustice and social untruth, the forest in which mankind has lost its way, make for us clearings and sunlit glades.

Our revolution was the work of the great bourgeois, of the men whose race is now extinct. They had their rude vices and their rude virtues. Contemporary civilisation has inherited their vices alone, their fanaticism and their greed. It is our hope that your revolution will be the uprising of a great people, hale, brotherly, humane, avoiding the excesses into which we fell.

Above all, remain united! Learn from our example. Remember how the French Convention, like Saturn, devoured its own children. Be more tolerant than we proved. Your whole strength will barely suffice for the defence of the sacred cause you represent; for its defence against the fierce and crafty enemies who at this hour perchance are arching their backs and purring like cats, but who are lurking in the jungle, awaiting the moment when you will stumble if you should be alone.

Last of all remember, Russian brothers, that you are fighting our battles as well as your own. Our fathers of 1792 wished to bring freedom to the whole world. They failed; and it may be that they did not choose the best way. But they had lofty ambitions. May these ambitions be yours likewise. Bring to Europe the gifts of peace and liberty!

"demain," Geneva, May 1, 1917.

VIII

TOLSTOY: THE FREE SPIRIT

IN his diary, of which the first French translation has just been issued by Paul Biriukov,[15] Tolstoy gives utterance to the fantasy that in an earlier life his personality had been a complex of loved beings. Each successive existence, he suggested, enlarged the circle of friends and the range and power of the soul.[16]

Speaking generally, we may say that a great personality comprehends within itself more souls than one. All these souls are grouped around one among them, much as, in a company of friends, the one with the strongest character will establish an ascendancy.

In Tolstoy there are more men than one: there is the great artist; there is the great Christian; there is the being of uncontrolled instincts and passions. But in Tolstoy, as his days lengthened and his kingdom extended, it became plain and yet more plain that there was one ruler. This ruler was the free reason. It is to the free reason that I wish to pay homage here, for it is this above everything that we all need to-day.

Our epoch is not poor in the other energies, those energies which Tolstoy possessed in so full a measure. Our age is surfeited with passions and with heroism; in artistic capacity it is not lacking; the fire of religion, even, has not been withheld. God—all the gods there be—have cast burning brands into the vast conflagration that rages among the nations. Christ not excepted. There is not one among the countries, belligerent or neutral, including the two Switzerlands, the

German and the Romance, which has failed to discover in the gospels justification for cursing or for slaughter.

Rarer to-day than heroism, rarer than beauty, rarer than holiness, is a free spirit. Free from constraint, free from prejudices, free from every idol; free from every dogma, whether of class, caste, or nation; free from every religion. A soul which has the courage and the straightforwardness to look with its own eyes, to love with its own heart, to judge with its own reason; to be no shadow, but a man.

To a surpassing degree, Tolstoy set such an example. He was free. Invariably, with steadfast gaze, he looked events and men in the face without blinking. His free judgment was unperturbed even by his affections. Nothing shows this more plainly than his independence towards the one whom he valued the most, towards Christ. This great Christian was not a Christian through obedience to Christ. Though he devoted a considerable part of his life to studying, expounding, and diffusing the gospels, he never said, "This or that is true because the gospels say so." Tolstoy's outlook was, "The gospels are true because they say this or that." You yourself must be the judge, your free reason must be the judge, of truth.

There is a writing known to few, for I believe it is still unpublished. It is the *Relation by Mihail Novikov the Peasant, concerning the Night of October 21, 1910, spent by him at Yasnaya Polyana*. The date was a week before Tolstoy fled from his home. We read how Tolstoy conversed at Yasnaya Polyana with a number of peasants. Among these were two village lads who had just been called up for military service, and military service was the topic of discussion. One of the young men, a social democrat, said that he was going to serve, not throne and altar, but state and nation. (We see that Tolstoy was fortunate in that he did not die before making the acquaintance of the "socialist patriots," before hearing a disquisition on "the art of turning the coat.") Some of the other peasants protested. Tolstoy enquired what were the limits of the state, declaring that for himself the whole world was his fatherland. The other conscript quoted texts from the Bible, texts in defence of killing. These did not convince Tolstoy, seeing that texts can be found apt for every occasion. He spoke as follows:

"Not because Moses or Christ has forbidden us to do ill to our neighbour or to ourselves, not for such a reason must we refrain from doing ill. It is our duty to refrain because it is contrary to the nature of man to do this ill either to himself or to his neighbour. Be careful to note that I say it is contrary to the nature of man. I am not speaking of beasts.... In yourself you must find God, that he may enable you to see what is good and what is evil, what is possible and what is impossible. But as long as we allow ourselves to be guided by an external authority, be it that of Moses and Christ for one man, that of Mohammed for another, and that of the socialist Marx for another, we shall not cease to be at enmity one with another."

I wish to make these words of power widely known. As I have repeatedly declared, the worst evil with which the world is afflicted is not the power of the wicked but the weakness of the good. Now this weakness is largely due to the inertia of the will, to the dread of independent judgment, to moral cowardice. The boldest, directly they have shaken off their chains, are only too ready to assume fresh bonds. Hardly have they been freed from one social superstition, than we see them deliberately harnessed to the chariot of a new superstition. It is so much easier to allow oneself to be guided than it is to think for oneself. This abdication is the kernel of the mischief. It is the duty of each one of us to refrain from leaving to others, to the best of men, to the most trustworthy, to the most dearly loved, the decision of what it is or is not good for us to do. We ourselves must seek the solution, seek it all through life if needs must, seek it with untiring patience. A half truth which we have won for ourselves is worth more than a whole truth learned from others, learned by rote as a parrot learns. A truth which we accept with closed eyes, submissively, deferentially, servilely—such a truth is nothing but a lie.

Stand erect! Open your eyes and look about you! Be not afraid! The modicum of truth which you can secure by your own efforts is your safest light. Your essential need is not the acquisition of vast knowledge. The essential is that the knowledge you gain, be it little or be it much, shall be your own, nourished with your own blood, outcome of your own untrammelled effort. Freedom of the spirit is the supreme treasure.

Throughout the ages, free men have been few in number. With the continued spread of herd mentality the number seems not unlikely to grow smaller yet. No matter! For the sake of these very multitudes who surrender to the slothful intoxication of collective passion, we must cherish the flame of liberty. Let us seek truth everywhere; let us cull it wherever we can find its blossom or its seed. Having found the seed let us scatter it to the winds of heaven. Whencever it may come, whithersoever it may blow, it will be able to germinate. There is no lack, in this wide universe, of souls that will form the good ground. But these souls must be free. We must learn not to be enslaved even by those whom we admire. The best homage we can pay to men like Tolstoy is to be free, as Tolstoy was free.

"Les Tablettes," Geneva, May 1, 1917.

IX

TO MAXIM GORKI

At Geneva, in January, 1917, A. V. Lunacharski delivered a lecture on the life and works of Maxim Gorki. The following tribute to Gorki was read before the lecture.

ABOUT fifteen years ago, in Paris, Charles Péguy, myself, and a few others, used to meet in a little ground-floor shop in the rue de la Sorbonne. We had just founded the "Cahiers de la Quinzaine." Our editorial office was poorly furnished, neat and clean; the walls were lined with books. A photograph was the only ornament. It showed Tolstoy and Gorki standing side by side in the garden at Yasnaya Polyana. How had Péguy got hold of it? I do not know, but he had had several reproductions made, and each of us had on his desk the picture of these two distant comrades. Under their eyes part of *Jean Christophe* was written.

One of the two men, the veteran apostle, has gone, on the eve of the European catastrophe whose coming he foretold and in which his voice has been so greatly needed. The other, Maxim Gorki, is at his post, and his free-spirited utterances help to console us for Tolstoy's silence.

Gorki has not proved one of those who succumbed to the vertigo of events. Amid the distressing spectacle of the thousands of writers, artists, and thinkers who, within a few days, laid down their role as guides and defenders of the masses, to follow the maddened herds, to drive these herds yet more crazy by their own cries, to hasten the rush into the abyss, Maxim Gorki was one of the rare exceptions, one of those whose reason and whose love of humanity remained unshaken. He dared to speak on behalf of the persecuted, on behalf of the gagged and enslaved masses. This great artist, who shared for so long the life of the unfortunate, of the humble, of the victims, of the outcasts of society, has never denied his sometime companions. Having become famous, he turns back to them, throwing the powerful light of his art into the dark places where wretchedness and social injustice are hidden away. His generous soul has known suffering; he does not close his eyes to the sufferings of others.

Haud ignara mali, miseris succurrere disco....

Consequently, in these days of trial (trial which we greet, because it has taught us to take stock of ourselves, to estimate the true value of hearts and of thoughts), in these days when freedom of the spirit is everywhere oppressed, we must cry aloud our homage to Maxim Gorki. Across the battlefields, across the trenches, across a bleeding Europe, we stretch forth our hands to him. Henceforward, in face of the hatred which rages among the nations, we must affirm the union of New Europe. To the fighting "Holy Alliances" of the governments, we counterpose the brotherhood of the free spirits of the world!

January 30, 1917.

"demain," Geneva, June, 1917.

X

TWO LETTERS FROM MAXIM GORKI

PETROGRAD, *end of December, 1916.*

My dear and valued comrade Romain Rolland,

WILL you be good enough to write a biography of Beethoven, suitable for children? I am simultaneously writing to H. G. Wells, whom I ask to let me have a life of Addison; Fridtjof Nansen will do the life of Christopher Columbus; I shall myself deal with the life of Garibaldi; the Hebrew poet Bialik will write the life of Moses. With the aid of the leading authors of our day I hope to produce a number of books for children, containing biographies of the leaders of mankind. The whole series will be issued under my editorship....

You know that in these days nothing needs our attention so much as young people. We grown-ups, we whose course is nearly run, are leaving a poor inheritance to our children, are bequeathing to them a sad life. This foolish war is a striking proof of our moral weakness, of the decay of civilisation. Let us, then, remind our children that men have not always been so weak and so bad as we are. Let us remind them that in all the nations there have been and still are great men, fine spirits. Now, above all, should we do this, when savagery and brutality are rife.... I beseech you, my dear Romain Rolland, to pen this biography of Beethoven, for I am convinced that no one can do it better than yourself....

I have read and reread the articles you have published during the war, and I take this opportunity of telling you that they have inspired me with profound respect and love for you. You are one of the rare persons whose soul has remained unaffected by the madness of this war. It is a delight to me to know that you have continued to cherish the best principles of humanity.... Allow me, from a great distance, to clasp you by the hand, dear comrade.

Maxim Gorki.

*

* *

At the end of January, Romain Rolland replied, accepting the proposal that he should rewrite the life of Beethoven for young people, and asking Gorki to indicate the length and the method of treatment. Was the book to be a causerie, or a plain statement of facts? Rolland suggested additional names for the series of biographies: Socrates; Francis of Assisi; representative figures of Asia.

. . . Will you permit me to make a friendly remark? I am a trifle uneasy as to some of the names mentioned in your letter, uneasy as to the effect upon children's minds. You propose to put before them such formidable examples as that of Moses. Your aim, obviously, is to impress on them the importance of moral energy, which is the source of all light. But it is not a matter of indifference whether this light be turned towards the past or towards the future. There is no lack of moral energy to-day. The quality abounds, but it is devoted to the service of an obsolete ideal, an ideal which oppresses and kills. I must admit that I am somewhat estranged from the great men of the past, considered as examples for the conduct of life. For the most part I am disappointed in them. I admire them on aesthetic grounds, but I cannot endure the intolerance and the fanaticism they so often display. Many of the gods whom they worshipped have to-day become dangerous idols. Mankind, I fear, will fail to fulfil its lofty destiny unless it can transcend these earlier ideals, unless it prove able to offer wider horizons to the coming generations. In a word, I love and admire the past; but I wish the future to excel the past. It can; it must....

*
* *

Maxim Gorki answered as follows:—

PETROGRAD, *March 18 to 21, 1917.*

I hasten to reply, dear Romain Rolland. The book on Beethoven should be written for young people from thirteen to eighteen years of age. It should be an objective and interesting account of the life of a man of genius, of the development of his mind, of the chief incidents in his career, of the difficulties he overcame and of the triumphs he achieved. It should contain as much as can be learned concerning Beethoven's childhood. In young folk we wish to inspire love for life and trust in life; to adults we wish to teach heroism. Man has to learn that he is the creator and the master of the world; that his is the responsibility for all its misfortunes; that his, too, is the credit for all that is good in life. We must help man to break the chains of individualism and nationalism. Propaganda on behalf of universal union is absolutely essential.

I am delighted with your idea of writing the life of Socrates, and I hope you will carry it out. I suppose your description of Socrates will be placed on a background of classical life, on the background of the life of Athens?

Most penetrating are your observations on the question of a life of Moses. I am entirely with you as far as concerns the disorganising influence which religious fanaticism exercises upon life. But I choose Moses simply as a social reformer. This will be the theme of his biography. I had thought of Joan of Arc. But I am afraid that the treatment of this topic would lead the writer to talk of "the mystical soul of the people," and of similar matters, which pass my understanding, and which are particularly unwholesome for Russians.

The life of Francis of Assisi is another story. It would be excellent, it would be extremely useful, if the writer of this biography were to aim at displaying the profound difference between Francis of Assisi and the holy men of the east, the saints of Russia. The east is pessimist; it is passive. The Russian saints do not love life; they repudiate it and execrate it. Francis is an epicure of religion; he is a Hellene; he loves God as the work of his own creation, as the fruit of his own soul. He is filled with love for life, and he is free from a humiliating fear of God. A Russian is a man who does not know how to live, but knows how to die.... I am afraid that Russia is even more oriental than China. We have a superabundant wealth of mysticism.... What we chiefly need to inspire men with is the love of action; we must awaken in them respect for the intelligence, for man, for life.

My sincerest thanks for your cordial letter. It is a great solace to know that somewhere, afar off, there is one who suffers the same sufferings as oneself, a man who loves the same things. It is good to know this in these days of violence and madness.... Warmest greetings.

MAXIM GORKI.

PS.—This letter has been delayed by recent happenings in Russia. Let us rejoice, Romain Rolland, let us rejoice with all our hearts, for Russia is no longer the mainspring of reaction in Europe. Henceforward the Russian people is wedded to liberty, and I trust that this union will give birth to many great souls for the glory of mankind.

"demain," Geneva, July, 1917.

XI

TO THE WRITERS OF AMERICA

Letter to "The Seven Arts," New York, October, 1916.

I AM delighted to learn of the creation of a magazine in which the American soul will become fully aware of its own individuality. I believe in the lofty destinies of America, and the events of the hour render the realisation of that destiny urgently necessary. In the Old World, civilisation is imperilled. America must cherish the flickering flame.

You possess one great advantage over us in Europe. You are free from traditions; free from the burdens of thought, of sentiments, from agelong follies, from the obsessions in the spheres of the intellect, of art, and of politics; you are free from all these things which crush the Old World. Contemporary Europe is sacrificing her future to quarrels, ambitions, rancours, revived again and again. Every endeavour to bring these troubles to an end serves but to add a few meshes to the net wherein a murderous destiny has snared us. Our fate resembles that of the Atrides, vainly awaiting, as in the *Eumenides,* a god's word of power which may break the bloody spell. In art, if our writers owe their perfection of form and their clarity of thought to the strength of our classical traditions, these advantages have been gained at the cost of great sacrifices. Too few among our artists are awakened to the manifold life of the world. Their minds are mewed within a closed garden. They display little interest concerning the spacious regions through which, after leaving that garden, the river, a swelling flood, pursues its torrential course, watering all the world.

You have been born in a land which is neither encumbered nor enclosed by the artificial constructions of the mind. Profit by the fact. Be free. Do not enslave yourselves to foreign examples. Your model is in yourselves. Begin by knowing yourselves.

This is the first duty. The differing individualities which combine to make up your country must not be afraid to express themselves in art; to express themselves freely, honestly, integrally; without straining for originality, but regardless of what expression may have been found by those who have gone before, and fearless of the tyranny of opinion. Above all, let them dare to look into their own souls, to look well and long, to plumb the depths in silent meditation. Those who do so, must then dare to reveal what they have seen. This self-communing is not a self-incarceration within an egoistic personality. Those who engage in it will strike deep roots in the essential being of the nation to which they belong. I urge on you the endeavour to participate to the full in its sufferings and its aspirations. Be the light lightening the darkness of the great social masses whose mission it is to renew the world. The men and women of the common people, those whose want of interest in artistic matters is often a trial to you, are mutes. Lacking power of expression, they are ignorant of themselves. Become a voice for them. As they hear you speak, they will grow aware of themselves. In giving expression to your own souls, you will create the soul of your nation.

Your second task, vaster and more distant, will be to form a fraternal link between these free individualities, to build a rose window that shall concentre their multiple trends, to compose a symphony from out their various voices. The United States is made up of elements drawn from all the nations of the world. Let the richness of the structure help you to understand the essence of all these nations, to realise the harmony of their intellectual energies!—To-day, in the Old World, we witness the deplorable and foolish antagonism displayed by national individualities, near neighbours and close kin, distinguished only by trifling shades like France and Germany, repudiating one another, longing for one another's destruction. Parochial disputes about which the human mind is eager to achieve self-mutilation! For my part I cry aloud, not merely that the intellectual ideal of a single nation is too narrow for me; I declare that the ideal of a reconciled western world would be too narrow for me; I declare that the ideal of a united Europe would still be too narrow for me. The hour has come in which man, truly healthy and truly alive, must deliberately turn his footsteps towards the ideal of a universal humanity, wherein the European races of the Old World and of the New will join hands with the representatives of the ancient and now rejuvenescent civilisations of Asia—of India and of China. A universal humanity with a common spiritual treasury. All these splendid types of mankind are mutually complementary. The thought of the future must be a synthesis of the great thoughts of the entire universe. America lies between the two oceans which lave the two continents; America is at the centre of the life of the world. Let it be the mission of all that is best in America to cement this fecund union!

To sum up, we ask of you two things, writers and thinkers of America. We ask, first of all, that you should defend freedom, that you should safeguard its conquests and extend them: political freedom and mental freedom, an unceasing renewal of life through freedom, through this great and ever-flowing river of the mind.

In the second place, we await from you that you should bring to pass, on behalf of the world, a harmony of diverse liberties; a symphonic expression of associated individualities, of associated races, of associated civilisations, of mankind at once integral and free.

You have splendid opportunities: you have an exuberant young life; you have wide areas of virgin land. Your day has just begun. You are not wearied by the toil of a previous day. You are unencumbered by the heritage of the past. All that comes down to you from the past is a voice like the sound of many waters, the voice of a great herald whose work seems a homeric foreshadowing of the task that awaits you. I speak of the American master, Walt Whitman.—Surge et age.

"Revue mensuelle," Geneva, February, 1917.

XII

FREE VOICES FROM AMERICA

I HAVE often deplored that during the war the Swiss press has failed to play the great part which was assigned to it. I have not hesitated to express my regret to Swiss journalists of my acquaintance. I do not reproach the Swiss periodicals for their lack of impartiality. It is natural, it is human, to have preferences, and to show them passionately. We have all the less reason to complain seeing that (at least among the Latin Swiss) the preferences are in our favour.

My chief grievance is that, since the beginning of the war, our Swiss friends have failed to keep us fully informed of what is going on around us. We do not ask a friend to judge for us; when we are carried away by passion, we do not ask him to be wiser than we are. But if he is in a position to see and know things that are hidden from us, we have a right to reproach him if he leaves us in ignorance. He does us wrong, for through his fault we are likely to fall into errors of judgment and are likely to act wrongly.

Neutral countries enjoy an inestimable advantage. They can look the problems of the war in the face, in a way that is utterly impossible to the belligerent nations. Above all, the neutrals enjoy the advantage of being able to speak freely, a piece of good fortune which they fail to esteem at its true value. Switzerland, in the very centre of the battlefield, between the fighting camps, with inhabitants drawn from three of the belligerent stocks, is peculiarly favoured. I have had occasion to perceive and to profit by the wealth of information at the disposal of the Swiss. Hither, from all parts of Europe, comes an abundance of news, evidence, printed matter.

Yet the Swiss press makes little use of this abundance. With few exceptions, Swiss periodicals are content to reproduce the official bulletins from the armies, and the semi-official statements issued by agencies that are open to suspicion, statements inspired by the governments or by the occult forces which to-day have far more governing power than the nominal heads of governments. Rarely do we find that the Swiss papers subject these interested statements to critical discussion. Hardly ever do we find contrasted views; hardly ever are we enabled to listen to independent voices from the opposing trenches.[17] Thus official truth, dictated by the powers that be, is imposed upon the masses with the potency of a dogma. Thought concerning the war has a catholicity which will not permit heresy to exist. Such a development is strange in Switzerland, and above all in this republic of Geneva, whose historic origins and whose reasons for existence were free opposition and fertilising heresy.

I do not propose to study the psychological causes of the suppression of thoughts which conflict with official dogma. I am inclined to think that partisan feeling is of less effect in this matter than, in some, ignorance of the facts and lack of critical faculty, and in others, really well-informed persons, failure to verify alleged facts, or an unwillingness to correct the errors of an overwrought public opinion—errors which, quite unknown to themselves, they really desire to believe. It is easier, and at the same time it is safer, to rest content with the news supplied from house to house by the great purveyors, rather than put oneself to the pains of going to the fountain head in order to revise or to supplement current information.

These errors and these lacunae are serious, however they originate, as the public is beginning to realise.[18] It is perfectly natural that the ideas of this or that social or political party, in one or other of the belligerent nations, should conflict with the ideas of this or that journal in a neutral land. No one need be surprised that such a neutral journal should openly express its dissent. Vigilant criticism would be equally in place. But it is not permissible that a neutral journal should ignore or distort everything of which it disapproves.

Is it not intolerable, for example, that we should know nothing about the Russian revolution except from news items issued from governmental sources (non-russian for the most part), or from hostile partisans eager to calumniate all the forward groups? Is it not intolerable that the great Swiss periodicals should never give an open platform to the persons thus vilified, not even in the case of such a man as Maxim Gorki, whose genius and intellectual candour are the glory of European letters? Once more, is it not intolerable that the French socialist minority should be systematically left out of the picture, should be regarded as non-existent by the journals of French-speaking Switzerland? Is it not monstrous that these same journals, during the last three years, have maintained absolute silence concerning the British opposition, or, if they have referred to it at all, have done so in the most contemptuous terms? For we have to remember that those who voice this opposition bear some of the greatest names in British thought, such as Bertrand Russell, Bernard Shaw, Israel Zangwill, Norman Angell, and E. D. Morel; we have to remember that its views find expression in vigorous periodicals, in numerous pamphlets, and in books some of which excel in value anything that during the same period has been written in Switzerland and in France!

Nevertheless, in the long run, the staying powers of the British opposition have got the better of national barriers; the thought of this opposition has made its way into France, where some of the leading spirits are now fully aware of this English work and of these English struggles. With regret I have to record that the Swiss press has played no part in promoting the mutual understanding, and I imagine that neither the French nor the British will forget the fact.

The same thing has happened in the United States of America. The Swiss periodicals have been delighted to publish whatever the powers that be have sent them for publication; but, as usual, the opposition has been forgotten or scoffed at. When by chance a semi-official telegram from New York, meticulously reproduced (unless it has been obligingly paraphrased and provided with a sensational headline), makes some reference to the opposition, it is only that we may be inspired with contempt. It would appear that any one on the other side of the Atlantic who proclaims himself a pacifist, even if it be on Christian grounds, is looked upon as a traitor, as working in the hire of the enemy. This no longer arouses our surprise. The experiences of the last three years have been such that nothing can now surprise us. But we have likewise lost all power of trust. Having learned that those who desire truth will vainly wait for it to come to them, we set out to seek truth for ourselves wherever it may be found. When there is no drinking water in the house, we must e'en go to the well.

To-day let us listen to the words of the opposition in America, as expressed by one of the boldest of the periodicals serving that movement, "The Masses" of New York.[19]

Here expression is given to non-official truth, and this, also, is no more than part of the truth. But we have the right to know the whole truth, be it pleasant or unpleasant. It is even our duty to know it, unless we are poltroons who fear to look reality in the face. You need not search the files of "The Masses" for records of greatness that has been lavished in the war! We know all about this, anyhow, from the official reports with which we are deluged. What we do not sufficiently know, what people do not wish to know, is the material and moral unhappiness, the injustice, the oppression which, as Bertrand Russell points out, are for each nation the obverse of every war, however just.—That is why, as far as America is concerned, we must consult the uncompromising periodical which I am about to quote.

*

* *

Max Eastman, the editor, is the soul of "The Masses." He fills it with his thought and his energy. The two last issues to reach me, those of June and July, 1917, contain no less than six articles from his pen. All wage implacable warfare against militarism and blind nationalism. Nowise duped by official declamations, Eastman declares that this war is not a war for democracy. The real struggle for liberty will come after the war.[20] In the United States, as in Europe, the war has been the work of capitalists, and of a group of intellectuals, clerical and lay.[21] Max Eastman insists on the part played by the intellectuals, whilst his collaborator John Reed emphasises the part played by the capitalists. Similar economic and moral phenomena have been apparent in the Old World and in the New. In the United States, as in Europe, many socialists support the war. A number of them (notably Upton Sinclair, with whom I am personally acquainted, and whose moral sincerity and idealist spirit I fully appreciate) have adopted this strange militarism. They champion universal conscription, in the hope that after the "war for democracy" "the socialist movement will know how to 'employ such a disciplined army' in building the co-operative commonwealth."[22]

As for the men of religion, they have rushed headlong into the fray. At a meeting of Methodist ministers in New York, one of them, a pastor from Bridgeport, Connecticut, straightforwardly declared, "If I must choose between my country and my God, I have made up my mind to choose God." He was hooted and threatened by the other members of the assembly, five hundred in number; was denounced as a traitor. Newel Dwight Hillis, preaching in the Henry Ward Beecher church, said: "All God's teachings concerning forgiveness must be abrogated as far as Germany is concerned. When the Germans have been shot I will forgive them their atrocities. But if we agree to forgive Germany after the war, I shall think that the world has gone mad."

Billy Sunday, a sort of howling dervish, sprung from heaven knows where, brays to huge crowds a militarist gospel. He spouts his sermons like a sewer disgorging filth; he calls upon the Good Old God (who is apparently to be found in other places besides Berlin), buttonholes him, enrols him willy-nilly. A cartoon of Boardman Robinson's shows Billy Sunday arrayed as a recruiting sergeant, dragging Christ by a halter and shouting: "I got him! He's plumb dippy over going to war." Fashionable folk, ladies included, are infatuated with this preacher; they delight to debase themselves in God's company. The ministers of religion, too, are on Billy Sunday's side. The exceptions may be counted on the fingers of one hand. Most notable among the exceptions is the pastor of the church of the Messiah in New York, John Haynes Holmes by name, from whom I had the honour of receiving a magnificent letter in February, 1917, just before the United States entered the war. In its July number "The Masses" published an admirable declaration issued by Holmes to his flock. It was entitled, What shall I do? He refuses to exclude any nation from the human community. The church of the Messiah will not respond to any militarist appeal. His conscience constrains him to refuse conscription. He will obey his conscience at any cost. "God helping me, I can no otherwise."—Those who resist the war madness constitute a little Church where persons of all parties make common cause, Christians, atheists, Quakers, artists, socialists, etc. Hailing from all points of the compass, and holding the most conflicting ideas, they share only one article of faith, that of the war against war. This common creed suffices to bring them into closer association than the associations they had with their friends of yesterday, with their brothers by blood, by religion, or by profession.[23] Thus did Christ pass to and fro among the men of Judea, detaching those who believed in him from their families, from their class, from all their past life.—In the United States, as in Europe, young men are far less possessed with the war spirit than their elders. A striking example comes from Columbia University. Here, while the professors were conferring on General Joffre the degree of doctor of literature, the students assembled to pass a unanimous resolution against answering the call of military conscription.[24] This exposed the voters to the penalty of imprisonment. For they manage things with a heavy hand in the classic land of liberty. Many American citizens have been thrown into gaol, and others, we are informed, have been immured in lunatic asylums, for having expressed their disapproval of the war. The recruiting sergeants go wherever they please, even forcing their way into meetings of the workers and maltreating all who resist them.[25] Under the rubric A Week's War "The Masses" records all the brutalities, all the blows, wounds, and murders, to which the war has already led in America. We may well ask to what extremes of violence these antipacifist repressions will some day be carried. The alleged freedom of speech in the United States would appear to be pure humbug. "In actual fact," exclaims Max Eastman, "freedom of speech has never existed." It is by law established. "But in practice there reigns a contempt for law, to the advantage of the strong and to the detriment of the weak." We have long known this through the revelations of the Italian and Russian socialist press, in connection with the scandalous sentences passed on working men. Do pacifists give trouble? They are arrested as anarchists! Does a periodical refuse to bow to the opinion of the state? It is suppressed without parley; or sometimes, by a more refined procedure, it is prosecuted for obscenity![26] And so on.

Max Eastman's chief collaborator, John Reed, endeavours to throw light on the preponderating role played by American capitalism in the war. In an article which adopts as title that of Norman Angell's book *The Great Illusion*, Reed declares that the pretence of fighting kings is maudlin, and that Money is the true king. Putting his finger on the sore spot, he adduces figures showing the colossal profits made by the great American companies. Under the bizarre title *The Myth of American Fatness*,[27] he shows that it is not, as Europe fancies, the American nation which battens on the war, but only two per cent of the population. Ninety-eight per cent of the inhabitants of the States are thin folk, and grow thinner daily. During the years 1912 to 1916, wages increased nine per cent, whilst the cost of food increased seventy-four per cent during the years 1915 and 1916. From 1913 to 1917, the general rise in prices was 85.32 per cent (flour 69 per cent, eggs 61 per cent, potatoes 224 per cent! Between January 1915 and January 1917, the rise in the price of coal was from $5 to $8.75 per ton). The bulk of the population has suffered cruelly, and serious hunger strikes have taken place in New York. Of course the European press has either said nothing about these or has ascribed them to German plots.

During the years 1914 to 1916, there occurred an increase of five hundred per cent in the dividends paid by twenty-four of the largest companies (steel, cast iron, leather, sugar, railways, electricity, chemical products, etc.). The dividend of the Bethlehem Steel Corporation rose from $5,122,703 in 1914 to $43,593,968 in 1916. The dividend of the United States Steel Corporation rose from $81,216,985 in 1914 to $281,531,730 in 1916. During the years 1914 and 1915, the number of wealthy persons in the United States increased as follows: From 60 to 120 in the case of those with a private income exceeding one million dollars; from 114 to 209 in the case of those with a private income ranging from half a million to one million dollars; while the number of those whose income ranged from one hundred thousand to half a million dollars was doubled.[28] In incomes below one hundred thousand dollars, there has been no notable increase. John Reed adds: "There are limits to the patience of the common people. Beware revolts!"

The first article in the July number of "The Masses" is a message to the citizens of the United States entitled *War and Individual Liberty*, penned by Bertrand Russell, the distinguished English philosopher and mathematician. It is dated February 21, 1917, prior to the U.S.

declaration of war, but could not be published before July. Russell recalls the self-sacrifice of the conscientious objectors in Britain, and the persecutions to which they have been exposed. He extols their faith (a faith for which he himself suffered). The cause of individual liberty is, he declares, the highest of all. Since the middle ages, the power of the state has grown unceasingly. It is now maintained that the state is entitled to dictate opinions to all, men and women. Prisons, emptied of criminals, who have been sent to the front in uniform to take part in the killing, are filled with honest men who refuse to be soldiers and to kill. A tyrannical society which has no place for rebels is a society condemned in advance. First of all its progress will be arrested, and then it will become retrogressive. The medieval church at least had, as counterpoise, the resistance of the Franciscans and of the reformers. The modern state has broken everything that resists its power; it has made around itself a void, an abyss wherein it will perish. Militarism is the modern state's instrument of oppression, just as dogma was the instrument of the church.—What is this state, before which all cringe? How absurd to speak of it as an impersonal authority, to invest it with a quasi-sacred character! The state consists of a few elderly gentlemen, for the most part of less than average ability, for they are cut off from the new life of the masses. Hitherto, the United States has been the freest of the nations. She has reached a critical hour, not for herself merely, but for the world at large, which regards her with tense anxiety. Let America beware. Even a just war may give rise to all possible iniquities. Vestiges of ancient fierceness linger within us; the human animal licks its chops as it watches the gladiatorial combats. We veil these cannibal appetites under highsounding names, speaking of Right and of Liberty. The last hope of our day lies in youth. Let youth claim for the future the individual's prerogative to judge good and evil for himself, to be the arbiter of his own conduct.

Side by side with these serious words, a large place, in the combat of thought, is given to humour, that bright and beauteous weapon. Charles Scott Wood writes amusing Voltairian dialogues. Here we see Billy Sunday in heaven, filling the place with clamour. He preaches a sermon full of Billingsgate, a sermon addressed to God, represented as an old gentleman with suave and distinguished manners, a little tired, speaking softly. St. Peter is instructed to enforce a new divine ordinance, for God, weary of the insipid company of simple souls, has decided that only persons of intelligence are to be admitted to paradise in future. Consequently no one killed in the war will pass the gate, except the Poles, who claim no merit for being sacrificed, but say they were sacrificed against their will.

Louis Untermeyer contributes poems. A number of excellent book reviews and several columns of theatrical criticism deal with questions of the hour. Among the works referred to, I may mention two of great originality: a book filled with bold paradox by Thorstein Veblen, entitled *Peace? An Inquiry into the Nature of Peace*; a Russian play in four acts by Artsibashev, *War*, depicting the cycle of the war in a family and the wastage of souls which it involves.

Finally we have vigorous drawings, the work of satirists of the pencil. R. Kempf, Boardman Robinson, and George Bellows, enliven the magazine with their pungent visions and their cutting words. Kempf shows us War crushing in his embrace France, England, and Germany, crying out: "Come on in, America, the blood's fine!" The four linked figures are dancing on a sea of blood in which corpses are floating.—A few pages further on, Boardman Robinson shows Liberty in the background weeping. In front stands Uncle Sam, wearing handcuffs (censorship) and leg-irons, the cannon-ball of conscription drags at the chain. He is described as being "All ready to fight for Liberty."—George Bellows' design depicts a chained Christ in prison. He is "incarcerated for the use of language calculated to dissuade citizens from entering the United States armies."—Finally, upon a heap of dead, the two sole survivors are seen savagely cutting one another to pieces. They are Turkey and Japan. The legend runs: "1920: still fighting for civilisation." This design is by H. R. Chamberlain.

*

* *

Thus fight, across the seas, a few independent spirits. Freedom, clearness, courage, and humour, are rare virtues. Still more rarely do we find them united, in days of folly and enslavement. In the American opposition, these virtues take the palm.

I do not pretend that the opposition is impartial. It, likewise, is influenced by passion, so that it fails to recognise the moral forces animating the other side. The combined wretchedness and greatness of these tragical days lies in the fact that both parties are drawn to the fight by lofty, though conflicting ideals, which endeavour to slay one another while volleying abuse at one another like Homer's heroes. We, at least, claim the right of doing justice even to our adversaries, even to the champions of the war which we loath. We know how much idealism, how much intense moral feeling, have been poured out on behalf of this sinister cause. We are aware that in this respect the United States has been no less spendthrift than Britain and France. But we wish people to give respectful hearing to the voices from the other side, from the peace party. Since the apostles of peace are few in number, since they are oppressed, they have all the more right to demand the esteem of the world. Everything rages against these bold men: the formidable power of the armed states; the baying of the press; the frenzy of blinded and drunken public opinion.

The world may howl as it pleases, may stop its ears as much as it likes; we shall compel the world to listen to these voices. We shall compel the world to pay homage to this heroic struggle, which recalls that of the early Christians against the Roman empire. We shall compel it to respect the brotherly greeting of such a man as Bertrand Russell, a new apostle Paul, "ad Americanos"; we shall compel the world to respect these men whose souls have remained free, these men who from their prisons in Europe and their prisons in America, clasp hands across the sea, and across the ocean that is yet wider than the Atlantic, the ocean of human folly.

August, 1917.

"demain," September, 1917.

XIII

ON BEHALF OF E. D. MOREL

E. D. Morel, secretary of the Union of Democratic Control, was arrested in London during August, 1917, and was sentenced to six months' imprisonment in the second division, upon the ridiculous (and incorrect) charge of having *attempted* to send to Romain Rolland in Switzerland one of his own political pamphlets which was being freely circulated in England.[29] The "Revue mensuelle" of Geneva asked R. R. what he thought of this affair, concerning which at that time little was known on the continent, for all the information hitherto published had been in the form of defamatory articles, attacks upon Morel manufactured in England and disseminated in various tongues. R. R. replied as follows:—

YOU ask what I think of the arrest of E. D. Morel.

I am not personally acquainted with E. D. Morel. I do not know whether, as is asserted, he has sent me some of his works during the war. I never received them.

But from all that I know of him, of his activities prior to the war, of his crusade against the crimes of civilisation in Africa, of his writings upon the war (few of which have been reproduced in Swiss or in French journals), I consider him to be a man of high courage and vigorous faith. He has always dared to serve truth, to serve truth alone, scorning danger, regardless of all the animus he was arousing. These things would be little. Morel has displayed rarer qualities, has achieved a more difficult task, in that he has been willing to disregard his own sympathies, his friendships, and even his country, when the truth and his country were at odds.

Thus he is in the succession of all the great believers: Christians of the early centuries, the reformers during the epoch of the wars of religion, the freethinkers of the heroic age of free thought, all those who have prized beyond everything their faith in truth—in whatever form truth presented itself to their minds (divine or human, for to them it was always sacred). I may add that such a man as E. D. Morel is a great citizen even when he is demonstrating to his country the errors which it is committing. Nay more, he is preeminently a great citizen when he does this and because he does it. Some would draw a veil over the errors of their country; they are unprofitable servants, or they are sycophants. Every brave man, every straightforward man, knows best how to honour his country.

The state may strike down such a man if it pleases, as the state struck down Socrates, as the state has struck down so many others, to whom, after they were dead, it raised useless monuments. The state is not our country. It is merely the administrator of our country, sometimes a good administrator, sometimes a bad one, but always fallible. The state has power, and uses power. But since man has been man, this power has invariably broken vainly against the threshold of the free soul.

R. R.

September 15, 1917.

"Revue mensuelle," Geneva, October, 1917.

XIV

YOUNG SWITZERLAND

IF we were to attempt to found our judgment upon Swiss periodical literature, we should form a very false opinion regarding the public mind of Switzerland. In this land, as everywhere, the press is from ten to twenty years behind the intellectual and moral development of the people. The Swiss papers and other periodicals are few in number, compared with those of neighbouring nations. Most of them are controlled by quite a small group of persons, and nearly every one of them serves to express the prejudices, the interests, and the routinism of middle-aged or elderly persons. Among such as are prominent in this journalistic world, even those who are spoken of as young, if they ever have been young in mind, are now so only in the eyes of their elders, of elders who refuse to admit that they have grown old.... "Young man, hold your tongue," as Job said to Magnus.[30]

A man may live a long time in this land before he discovers the existence of a young Switzerland free from the trammels of conservative liberalism (more conservative than liberal), and free from those of sectarian radicalism (preeminently sectarian). Both these trends are abundantly represented in the columns of the leading newspapers; the adherents of both are attached to the outworn political and social forms of the bourgeois regime which is declining from one end of Europe to the other.

I was surprised and delighted at what I read in the latest issues of the "Revue de la Société de Zofingue." I wish to make my French friends acquainted with what I have learned, so that sympathetic relationships may be established between them and young Switzerland.

The Zofingia Society is the leading society of Swiss students, and the oldest. It was founded in 1818, and will therefore celebrate its centenary next year. It comprises twelve sections: nine of these are "academic," viz. Geneva, Lausanne, Neuchâtel, Berne, Basle, and Zurich; three are "gymnasial," viz. St. Gall, Lucerne, and Bellinzona.[31] The membership of the society is steadily increasing. In July, 1916, it was 575; but now, nearly a year later, it is 700. The organisation has a monthly review, "Centralblatt des Zofingervereins," issued in French, German, and Italian. This periodical is now in its fifty-seventh year. It publishes lectures, reports of discussions, and other matters of interest to the association.

The essential distinction between this body and the other societies of Swiss students is that the Zofingia, as explained in the first article of its constitution, "places itself above and outside all political parties, but takes its stand on democratic principles.... It abstains entirely from party politics." Thus, as its president writes, it affords to the students of Switzerland a permanent possibility of creating anew and ever anew their conception of "the true national spirit of Switzerland.... In it, each generation can freely think out for itself fresh ideals, can construct new forms of life. Thus the history of the Zofingerverein is something more than a history of a Swiss students' club; it is a miniature history of the moral and political evolution of Switzerland since 1815."—But it has always been in the vanguard.

This society, drawing its members from three races and nine cantons, exhibits, as may be imagined, multiplicity in unity. The "Centralblatt" for November, 1916, contains a report of the year 1915-16, compiled by Louis Micheli. It gives an account of the activities of the various sections, and skilfully indicates the peculiar characteristics of each section.

The most important section, the one which leads the Zofingia, is that of Zurich. Here the problems of the hour are discussed with especial eagerness. Centring round opposite poles, there are two parties, substantially equal in numbers, and inspired with equal enthusiasm. On the one hand we see conservatives, authoritarian and centralist in trend, the devotees of "Studententum" of the old style. At the other pole are the young Zofingians whose outlook is socialistic, idealistic, and revolutionary. For a time there was a fierce struggle between these two groups. The parties succeeded one another in power, and those who gained control in one term would seek to undo everything which during the preceding term had been done by the members of the late committee. Now, a more conciliatory spirit prevails.[32] The progressive party, reinforced by a number of youthful recruits, has gained the upper hand. It is endeavouring to secure wider support by attracting additional elements through breadth of view and a policy of toleration.[33] But we are told that "the Zurichers, at bottom, are not strongly individualist, for they are apt to immolate their individuality on the altar of party. Hence there is danger, from time to time, that a revival of absolutism may take place."

At Basle, it would seem, there is no such danger. This section, the largest, extremely alert, is perhaps the least united and the most discordant. During the last few years it has been torn by dissensions aroused by the question of patriotism, but its members are not, like those of the Zurich section, grouped in two armies. There are a number of little factions, circumscribed and mutually suspicious. Its most conspicuous traits are the following. Its discussions are conducted with much bitterness, so that "there is a strong tendency for differences in the realm of ideas to culminate in personal hostility." The Baslers have little inclination towards practical activities; they prefer abstract discussions; they aim at the development of character and individuality. "In these respects, Basle and Lausanne are the sections containing the most original and individual types." But, in contrast with Lausanne, the Basle section has little interest in literary and artistic questions.

In the Lausanne section, individual types abound. Here we find students of the most various temperaments, and interested in the most diverse questions, in politics, sociology, literature, and the arts. But Lausanne is pugnacious, and is on bad terms with the other sections. It is itself broken up into factions, and it exhibits separatist trends, which led to a crisis early in 1916. After the manner of Vaud, it keeps itself to itself.

Lausanne, Basle, and Zurich are the three largest sections.

Lucerne and Berne are the smallest. In the former, which is of little importance, a "slothful cordiality" prevails. The Berne section is sleepy as well as small, with very few new adherents. One of its members has stigmatised Berne as a "Beamtenstadt" (civil servants' town). The Berne section has little interest in the problems of modern life, its attachments are to common sense; it is material and unemotional; it favours the established order. "The Bernese, by nature, distrusts innovators and idealists, regarding them as dreamers or revolutionists.... The state of mind of the Berne students recalls that which prevails in official circles."

St. Gall, hard-working, enthusiastic, and independent, occupies an intermediate position. "In St. Gall, every one can express his opinion frankly"; but the section is unimportant compared with Zurich or Basle.—Neuchâtel displays fitful energy, and "is fundamentally characterised by a certain natural inertia."—Geneva, finally, is amorphous. "The bulk of the members of this section make up a slumbrous, irresolute mass of persons who never utter any definite opinions," and perhaps have no definite opinions. Such activities as it displays are the work of a few exceptions. "No section has greater need of a masterful president." Having no leader, it is vague, somnolent, and takes little interest in current events. It lacks the corporate spirit. "The Genevese are strongly individualistic, and yet, unfortunately, we rarely find among them a strong individuality." We may add that they continue to display certain characteristics of the Genevese of old. Dreading criticism and ironical comment, they are afraid to let themselves go, to show what they really feel; their sensibilities are easily wounded, and they therefore invest themselves with coldness as with a cuirass; their attitude is one of perpetual mistrust; they are ever on the defensive, as if the duke of Savoy were always on the point of storming the walls.[34]

I pass no judgments. I am merely registering, in brief, the opinions of those among the students who are best qualified to judge. Taking them all in all, these opinions harmonise with my own observations.

*

* *

The latest issues of the "Centralblatt des Zofingervereins" manifest a free spirit. The issue for May, 1917, contains a frankly internationalist article by Jules Humbert-Droz entitled *National Defence*. Special mention must be made of a broad-minded lecture, *Socialism and the War*, delivered in February, 1917, by Ernest Gloor of Lausanne at the spring festival in Yverdon, and published in the "Centralblatt" for April and May. I must also refer to Gloor's lecture *What is our Country?*, delivered at Grütli in the canton of Lausanne. Another noteworthy lecture is that of Serge Bonhôte, delivered at Grütli in the canton of Neuchâtel, entitled *Fatherland*, and heralding the days to come. These lectures were respectively published in December, 1916, and January, 1917. I should have liked to give extracts from various appreciative articles upon *The Russian Revolution*. Above all, I should like to quote, from the April issue, Max Gerber's enthusiastic welcome to the revolution. But space is limited, and the best way of expounding the ideas of these young people will be to summarise a detailed discussion in which they have recently been engaged concerning *The Imperialism of the Great Powers and the Role of Switzerland*. The topic was suggested to the sections by Julius Schmidhauser of Zurich, "cand. jur.," president of the central section. Schmidhauser has edited the report of these discussions, bringing to the task a broad and tolerant synthetic spirit. The work is all the more remarkable seeing that it was penned during an arduous term of military service, when the man who signs himself "cand. jur." (law student) was playing the part of infantry lieutenant.

I shall merely follow his report, and shall allow the young men to speak for themselves. (Issues of March, April, and May, 1917).

The discussion comprises a preamble and six parts:

Preamble: How shall we envisage the Problem?

I. The Essence of Imperialism;

II. The Imperialism of the Great Powers to-day;

III. Can Imperialism be Justified?

IV. Opposition between the genuinely Swiss Outlook and the Imperialist Outlook.

V. The Mission of Switzerland;

VI. The new Education.

Preamble: How shall we envisage the Problem?

A. FROM THE REALIST OUTLOOK?

a. Can we explain imperialism as a historical product? This method is too easy-going; it is slothful and dangerous. "Should man be the creation of history? No; he should be its creator."—The condemnation of historical fatalism.

b. Can we explain imperialism by "Realpolitik"? Even if it be thus explicable, it must be no less energetically condemned. "I am inclined to define the 'real politicians' as persons who are marching along with their eyes closed to the essential realities of the world and of mankind.... 'Real politics' may often seem to be right for a season; but in the long run it always proves to have been wrong.... The war that rages to-day is the outcome of the deadly falsehood of 'real politics.' The motto of 'real politics,' which is 'si vis pacem, para bellum,' has been pushed to an absurdity, and has thus brought disaster upon our race. It is depressing to find that we are still afflicted with this curse. The only possible explanation of the sway which the doctrine of 'real politics' holds over so many minds is that such persons are fundamentally sceptical as to the reality of the good, the divine, in man" (Schmidhauser).

B. FROM THE UTILITARIAN OUTLOOK?

Certain persons are willing to fight some particular imperialism because it is or may be dangerous to Switzerland, while none the less they favour other imperialisms. The Zofingia must censure such a trend in the strongest terms. It is doubtless of urgent importance that we should take our stand against the first-named imperialism, but we must proscribe all the imperialisms. "Our aim is the attainment of a universally human outlook" (H. W. Lôw, of Basle).

C. From the Idealist Outlook??

This is no better than the others. The Zofingia denounces the hypocritical ideology of to-day, an ideology which serves to cloak a policy of brute interest. It desires to issue a warning against the other dangers of an abstract idealism, against the idealism of those who fail to derive their ideas from the unbiassed study of reality. One who locks himself up within the circle of his own ideas, one who opposes empty thought to life, one who claims the right of issuing absolute judgments (all or nothing) without regard to circumstances and ignoring the manifold shades of reality, exhibits dangerous pride and culpable levity.

D. Synthesis of the Foregoing Outlooks.

Realism without idealism has no sense. Idealism without realism has no blood. Genuine idealism wants life as a whole, desires its integral realisation. It is the deepest possible knowledge of living reality, simultaneously embracing human consciousness and facts. Such knowledge is our best weapon.

Part One.

The Essence of Imperialism.

The chief characteristic of imperialism is the will to power, the desire for expansion, the longing for domination. It is based upon a belief that might is right; it tends to impose itself by force. One of its mainsprings is the nationalist spirit, the mystical cult of nationality, of the chosen people; the sacred egoism of the fatherland. Never before has imperialism been so savage and unscrupulous as it has become to-day, owing to the economic conditions of contemporary society. "Imperialism is the inseparable companion of capitalism. In each country, capitalism requires as its main prop a vigorous and powerful state which can enter into successful competition with the capitalism of any other country. We give the name of imperialism to the tendency towards capitalistic and political expansion, which strides across frontiers" (Guggenheim). "Modern imperialism issues from the capitalist system dominating contemporary politics and society to-day. It is the cause of the world war" (Grob).

PART TWO.

The Imperialism of the Great Powers To-Day.

The central section of the Zofingia declares: "The imperialist character of the great powers engaged in the present struggle is indisputable." No objections are raised by the other sections. They unite in the view that "all the great powers pursue an imperialist policy."

Schmidhauser, presiding over the discussion, asks for justice towards the nations, for every one of them is, as it were, entangled in the net of the imperialist policy of Europe. He protests against the prejudiced and superficial outlook of those who can see nothing but the worst of any nation: of those who in the case of Germany concentrate attention on the spirit of a Treitschke or a Bernhardi and on the crime of the occupation of Belgium; of those who in the case of England can see nothing but the policy of Joseph Chamberlain and Cecil Rhodes, nothing but the Boer War. The mission of Switzerland is to realise the tragedy of mankind as a whole, and not to identify herself with any particular section of humanity. "Childish and stupid are the views of those for whom half of Europe should be placed in the pillory, while the other half should wear the aureole of all the virtues and all the heroisms" (Patry).

PART THREE.

Can Imperialism be Justified?

A. THE CHAMPIONS OF IMPERIALISM.

In only one section, that of Basle, does imperialism find defenders. Walterlin takes up his parable on its behalf, glorifying it in the spirit and the style of Nietzsche. "Imperialism," he declares, "is the artery of the world, the sole source of greatness, the creator of all progress." ...

B. THE OPPONENTS OF IMPERIALISM.

Opposition to imperialism is voiced by all the other sections. Most of them are content to show that imperialism is a menace to Switzerland, but Schmidhauser is by no means satisfied with this narrow and selfish outlook. He explains the material and moral disasters which necessarily result from imperialism, and from its offspring, the world war. Imperialism destroys civilisation. It saps morality and law, the two things upon which human society is founded. It is hostile to three fundamental ideas: to the idea of the unity of mankind; to the idea of individuality; to the idea that every individual should have the right of self-determination.

PART FOUR.

Opposition between the genuinely Swiss Outlook and the Imperialist Outlook.

The existence of this opposition is admitted, as a matter of principle, by all the participants in the discussion. But difficulties arise when they come to consider the policy which Switzerland should in particular pursue. "What are we entitled to speak of as peculiarly and primitively Swiss?" (Patry).

A beginning is made by defining the political essence of Switzerland, stress being laid, first upon the basic neutrality of the country, and secondly upon its supra-national character. "The ideal of Switzerland," says Clottu, "is that of a nation established above and outside the principle of nationality." Thirdly, stress is laid upon the right to the free development of every individual and of every social group. A fourth characteristic of Switzerland is that in that country, before authority and before the law, there exists a democratic equality of all citizens, communities, cantons, nationalities, languages, etc. By its very essence, therefore, Switzerland is absolutely opposed to the imperialism of the great powers. "The victory of the imperialist principle would be the political death of Switzerland" (Guggenheim).

What is to be done? These young men are convinced that Switzerland has a mission, and are none the less aware that

Switzerland lacks capacity to fulfil that mission. With ingratiating modesty, they disclaim any desire "to play the pharisees to Europe." Whilst they believe in the excellence of the principles which underlie the Switzerland of their dreams (though not Switzerland as she exists to-day), "we must not suppose," says Patry, "that this is a fresh instance of the monopolisation of the Good and the Beautiful by a single country, which will become the only fatherland of these graces." We must be content with knowing that the ground is made ready for building, and that there is still plenty of work to be done.

"Now, at this very hour, the destiny of Switzerland stands revealed. At a time when the principle of nationality dominates the European situation with the strength of demoniacal possession, at a time when opposing civilisations are rending one another, our little state claims the honour of possessing a national ideal which dominates the nationalities and takes them all to its bosom. Does this seem like madness? Perhaps it does, to the sapient sceptic for whom the vision of the present masks the vision of the future. But it is not madness for those who are truly wise, for those who know that the great causes of the world have ever at the outset been nailed to the cross. The principle of nationality was a power for good in its own day. But if it has ceased to be a factor of freedom and toleration, if it has become the source of hatred, the source of blind and limitless national selfishness, then it is working for its own destruction. It is the mission of Switzerland to pave the way for a saner application of the principle of nationality" (Clottu).

"In this domain we can and should be conquerors. Owing to the historical origin of our country, owing to the fact that Switzerland comprises three races and three tongues, we foreshadow on a small scale the United States of Europe; in a word, we practise internationalism" (Patry).

Switzerland champions the right of the nations and champions democratic thought, as against imperialism, which is, fundamentally, an aristocratic reaction. Imperialism makes use of democracy, but enslaves it; it undermines the democratic pillars of modern states; it centralises all power in the hands of a single government. "We are reviving the age of the dictators, and there is a tragic irony in this at a time when the whole world is speaking of liberty and when the whole world is enslaved.... Down with imperialism, which turns the nations aside from their true destinies!"

"The size of our country matters little, provided that it has right and truth on its side.... We know that what New Switzerland has hitherto done is inadequate.... But a sacred fire is beginning to burn in our land.... Switzerland is a highway leading towards the future.... We are animated and united by a sublime conviction, by the feeling that we are the bearers of a great truth" (Schmidhauser).

PART FIVE.

The Mission of Switzerland.

"Switzerland can achieve greatness through principle alone. The only conquests permissible to Switzerland, are conquests in the realm of ideas" (Clottu).

We are not concerned here solely with the duty of a choice group of intellectuals. The questions at issue affect the people at large, those to whose service these young men have devoted themselves. A new spirit, an active faith, are requisite. The war has brought to light the weak spot in the Swiss character. Touching is the shame felt by these truehearted youths owing to the attitude of their country at the outset of the war. They are personally hurt by such surrenders of principle. In the strongest terms they censure the abdication of the Swiss soul at the time when Belgium was being invaded, noting with pain the absence of any national and public protest. But now there is a change of spirit. "We have a young and virile movement, the movement of those who are not satisfied with the mere existence of Switzerland, but who desire that Switzerland should prove herself worthy to exist, by her moral greatness and by helping to bring salvation to other peoples" (Schmidhauser). "The recognition of this duty will regenerate our national life" (Genevese section).

The practical difficulties are enormous, and must be frankly faced. Switzerland is in danger of being crushed in twofold fashion—military and economic. The fate of Belgium and the fate of Greece are plain warnings. She cannot forego her army, for this is a necessary safeguard of the ideal she represents. But this army, however large, does not and cannot suffice to avert economic pressure, which is an inevitable outcome of the existing system of society. We have, therefore, to draw the fatal conclusion that Switzerland is doomed should capitalist imperialism endure. For Switzerland neither can nor ought to come to terms with either group of allied powers. To take such a step would be to pass sentence of death upon herself. "Her existence is inseparably associated with the victory of the ideas of supra-national solidarity, of world-wide socialism, world-wide individualism, world-wide democracy." Grob boldly affirms: "To imperialist immoralism, with the device, 'Our interest is our right,' we counterpose, 'Right is our interest.'"

What are the leading tasks of Switzerland?

They are three: the universalisation of socialism; the universalisation of individualism; the universalisation of democracy.

1. World-wide Socialism.—The germ of this appears in the supra-national union which is the essential characteristic of Switzerland. But the young Zofingians are under no illusions, and they frankly denounce the faults of their own people. "We are far from being a nation of brothers. ...Our nation is divided: it is rent asunder by egoisms and imperialisms.... For every strong man who misuses his strength and his wealth, displays the spirit of imperialism" (A. de Mestral). This scourge must be vigorously combated. How? "By direct struggle with capitalism," says one (Alexander Jaques of Lausanne). "By organising solidarity," says another (Ernest Gloor of Lausanne). But the Swiss are fast bound, willy-nilly, to the social system of other nations, "to the international system of economic imperialism, the most abominable of all the internationalisms." It is therefore categorically incumbent upon the Swiss to devote themselves to furthering an active internationalism of social solidarity. They must enter into an understanding with anti-imperialists throughout the world. "It is necessary to promote the formation of an international group organised for the struggle against imperialist, absolutist, and materialist principles, simultaneously, in every land" (Châtenay).

2. World-wide Individualism.—We require a counterpoise to sociocracy. We must beware of any organisation, be it internationalist or pacifist, which claims to subjugate and atrophy the living forces of man. The political ideal is a genuine federalism which shall respect individualisms. As the old saying has it: Let everything be after its kind!

3. World-wide Democracy.—In this matter the students display perfect unanimity, for they have absolute faith in democracy. But with their customary scrupulousness, their dread of pharisaism, they admit that Switzerland is still far from being a true democracy. "To-day democracy is purely formal; in our own time the principle of true democracy is, in a sense, revolutionary."

They tell us some of their aspirations. They desire the democratic control of foreign policy. They want pacifism on a democratic basis. Almost universally in Europe, political power is in the control of a handful of men who embody imperialist egoism. The people must share this power. Each nation has the right to control its own destinies, in accordance with its own ideas and the dictates of its own will.

But once more, no illusions! With a clear-sightedness which is rare at this hour, these young men point out that "imperialism has become democratic," saying: "The western democracies, closely examined, are nothing more than the sovereignty of a capitalist and landowning caste."

The Russian revolution arouses new hopes. "The spectacle of the struggle between the two democratic revolutions in Russia, one capitalist and imperialist, the other anti-imperialist and socialist, illuminates the problem of democracy and imperialism. This spectacle shows the Swiss democracy its path and its mission." Above all, let Switzerland reject the new evangel, made in Germany, of a democracy supine before the will of a politico-economic power, a democracy which tends in home policy to class rule, and in foreign policy to imperialism! "We need a new orientation which shall deliver democratic thought from national restrictions, and from the sinister contemporary trend towards the reign of material force."

True democracy, supra-national democracy, must take its stand against "imperialism masquerading as democracy."

PART SIX.

The New Education.

This lengthy discussion leads up in the end to practical conclusions. Public education must be reorganised and must work in a new direction. The extant educational system suffers from a threefold inadequacy. 1. From the humanist point of view, it immures the mind in the study of remote epochs and past civilisations, and does nothing to prepare the pupil for the fulfilment of contemporary duties. 2. From the specifically Swiss point of view, it aims at creating a blind patriotism, which can neither enlighten nor guide the understanding; it monotonously reiterates the story of wars, victories, and brute force, instead of teaching liberty, instead of inculcating the lofty Swiss ideal; it cares nothing for the moral and material needs of the people of to-day. 3. From the technical point of view, it is abjectly materialist and militarist, and has no ideals. True, that there is a contemporary movement, and a strong one, in favour of what is called "national education," in favour of "the teaching of civics." But we must be on our guard! Here is a new peril. They would make a sort of state idol, despotic and soulless; they would make a state superstition, a state egoism, to which our minds are to be enslaved. Do not let us stoop to the lure. An immense task lies before us, and the Zofingerverein must lead the way. It must play its part in the fulfilment of the moral and intellectual mission of Switzerland. But not by isolating itself. It must never lose its feeling of solidarity of thought and action with other lands. It sends forth deeply-felt greeting to the "Gesinnungsfreunde," to the friends and companions in belligerent lands, to those young men who have fallen in France and in Germany, and to those who yet live. It must make common cause with them; it must work shoulder to shoulder with the free youth of the world. Julius Schmidhauser, president of the Zofingia, who chaired these discussions and subsequently summarised them, concludes with an Appeal to Brothers, an appeal to them that they shall have faith, that they shall act, that they shall seek new roads for a new Switzerland—for a new humanity.

*

* *

I have thought well to efface myself behind these students. Were I to substitute my thought for theirs, I should lay myself open to the reproach which I so often address to my generation. I have let them speak for themselves. Any commentary would detract from the beauty of the sight of these enthusiastic and serious young people, in this most tragical hour of history, discussing their duties ardently and at great length, taking stock of their faith, and solemnly affirming that faith in a sort of oath of the tennis court.[35] We see them affirming their faith in liberty; in the solidarity of the peoples; in their moral mission; in their duty to destroy the hydra of imperialism, both militarist and capitalist, whether at home or abroad; in their duty to construct a juster and more humane society.

I give them fraternal greetings. They do not speak alone. Everywhere the echoes answer. Everywhere I see young people resembling them, and stretching forth friendly hands to their fellows in Switzerland. The vicissitudes of this war—a war which, endeavouring to crush free spirits, has but succeeded in making them feel the need for seeking one another out and for cementing unity—has brought me into close relationships with the young of all countries, in Europe, in America, and even in the east and the far east. Everywhere I have found the same communion of sufferings and hopes, the same aspirations, the same revolts, the same determination to break with the past whose malevolence and stupidity have been so plainly proved. I have found them all animated with the same ambition to rebuild human society upon new foundations, wider and more firmly laid than those which sustain the quaking edifice of this old world of rapine and fanaticism, of savage nationalities scorched by the war, rearing heavenward frames blackened by the fire.

June, 1917.

"demain," Geneva, July, 1917.

XV

UNDER FIRE

BY HENRI BARBUSSE[36]

HERE we have a pitiless mirror of the war. In that mirror the war is reflected day by day for sixteen months. It is a mirror of two eyes; they are clear, shrewd, perspicacious, and bold; they are the eyes of a Frenchman. The author, Henri Barbusse, dedicates his book: "To the memory of the comrades who fell by my side at Crouy and on Hill 119," during December, 1915. In Paris *Le Feu* was honoured with the Goncourt prize.

By what miracle has so truth-telling a work been able to appear unmutilated, at a time when so many free words, infinitely less free, have been censored? I shall not attempt to explain the fact, but I shall profit by it. The voice of this witness drives back into the shadow all the interested falsehoods which during the last three years have served to idealise the European slaughter-house.

*

* *

The work is of the first rank, and is so full of matter that more than one article would be requisite to present its whole scope. All that I shall attempt to deal with here will be the chief aspects—its artistry and its thought.

The dominant impression it conveys is one of extreme objectivity. Save in the last chapter, wherein Barbusse expounds his ideas on social questions, we do not make the author's acquaintance. He is there among his obscure companions; he struggles and suffers with them, and from one moment to another his disappearance seems imminent; but he has the spiritual strength which enables him to withdraw himself from the picture and to veil his ego. He contemplates the moving spectacle, he listens, he feels, he touches; he seizes it, with all his senses on the stretch. Marvellous is the assured grasp displayed by this French spirit, for no emotion affects the sharpness of the outline or the precision of the technique. We discern here manifold touches, lively, vibrant, crude, well fitted to reproduce the shocks and starts of the poor human machines as they pass from a weary torpor to the hyperaesthesia of hallucination—but these juxtaposed touches are placed and combined by an intelligence that is ever master of itself. The style is impressionist. The author is prone, unduly prone in my opinion, to make use of visual word-plays after the manner of Jules Renard. He is fond of "artistic writing," a typically Parisian product, a style which in ordinary times seems to "powder puff" the emotions, but which, amid the convulsions of the war, exhibits a certain heroic elegance. The narrative is terse, gloomy, stifling; but there come episodes of repose, which break its unity, and by these the tension is relieved for a moment. Few readers will fail to appreciate the charm, the discreet emotion, of these episodes, as for instance in the chapter "On Leave." But three-fourths of the book deal with the trenches of Picardy, under the "muddy skies," under fire and under water—visions now of hell, now of the flood.

There the armies remain buried for years, at the bottom of an eternal battlefield, closely packed, "chained shoulder to shoulder," huddling together "against the rain which descends from the skies, against the mud which oozes from the ground, against the cold, an emanation from the infinite which is all-pervading." The soldiers uncouthly rigged out in skins, rolls of blanket, ... cardigans, and more cardigans, squares of oilcloth, fur caps, ... hoods of tarpaulin, rubber, weatherproof cloth ... look like cave men, gorillas, troglodytes. One of them, while digging, has turned up an axe made by quaternary man, a piece of pointed stone with a bone handle, and he is using it. Others, like savages, are making rough ornaments. Three generations side by side; all the races, but not all the classes. Sons of the soil and artisans for the most part. Small farmers, agricultural labourers, carters, porters and messengers, factory foremen, saloon keepers, newspaper sellers, ironmongers' assistants, miners—very few liberal professions are represented. This amalgam has a common speech, "made up of workshop and barrack slang and of rural dialects seasoned with a few neologisms." Each one is shown to us as a silhouette, a sharp and admirable likeness; once we have seen them we shall always know them apart. But the method of depiction is very different from that of Tolstoi. The Russian cannot meet with a soul without plumbing it to the depths. Here we look and pass on. The individual soul hardly exists; it is a mere shell. Beneath that shell, the collective soul, suffering, overwhelmed with fatigue, brutalised by the noise, poisoned by the smoke, endures infinite boredom, drowses, waits, waits unendingly. It is a "waiting-machine." It no longer tries to think; "it has given up the attempt to understand, it has renounced being itself." These are not soldiers, they don't wish to be soldiers, they are men. "They are men, good fellows of all kinds, rudely torn away from life; they are ignorant, not easily carried away, men of narrow outlook, but full of common sense which sometimes gets out of gear. They are inclined to go where they are led and to do as they are bid. They are tough, and able to bear a great deal. Simple men who have been artificially simplified yet more, and in whom, by the force of circumstances, the primitive instincts have become accentuated: the instinct of self-preservation, egoism, the dogged hope of living through, the lust of eating, drinking, and sleeping." Even amid the dangers of an artillery attack, within a few hours they get bored, yawn, play cards, talk nonsense, "snatch forty winks"—in a word, they are bored. "The overwhelming vastness of these great bombardments wearies the mind." They pass through a hell of suffering and forget all about it. "We've seen too much, and everything we saw was too much. We are not built to take all that in. It escapes from us in every direction; we are too small. We are forgetting-machines. Men are beings which think little; above all, they forget." In Napoleon's day every soldier had a marshal's baton in his knapsack, and every soldier had in his brain the ambitious image of the little Corsican officer. There are no longer any individuals now, there is a human mass which is itself lost amid elemental forces. "More than six thousand miles of French trenches, more than six thousand miles of such miseries or of worse; and the French front is only one-eighth of the whole." Instinctively the narrator is compelled to borrow his images from the rough mythology of primitive peoples, or from cosmic convulsions. He speaks of "rivers of wounded torn from the bowels of the earth which bleeds and rots unendingly"—"glaciers of corpses"—"gloomy immensities of Styx"—"Valley of Jehoshaphat"—prehistoric spectacles. What does the individual man amount to in all this? What does his suffering mean? "What's the use of complaining?" says one wounded man to another. "That's what war is, not the battles, but the terrible unnatural weariness; water up to the middle, mud, filth, infinite monotony of wretchedness, interrupted by acute tragedies."—At intervals, human groans, profound shudders, issue from the silence and the night.

Here and there, in the course of this long narration, peaks emerge from the grey and bloody uniformity: the attack ("under fire"); "the field hospital"; "the dawn." I wish I had space to quote the admirable picture of the men awaiting the order to attack; they are motionless; an assumed calm masks such dreams, such fears, such farewell thoughts! Without any illusions, without enthusiasm, without excitement, "despite the busy propaganda of the authorities, without intoxication either material or moral," fully aware of what they are doing, they await the signal to hurl themselves "once more into this madman's role imposed on each of them by the madness of mankind." Then comes the "headlong rush to the abyss," where blindly, amid shell-splinters hissing like red-hot iron plunged into water, amid the stench of sulphur, they race forward. Next comes the butchery in the trenches, where "at first the men do not know what to do," but where a frenzy soon seizes them, so that "they hardly recognise those whom they know best, and it seems as if all their previous life had suddenly retreated to a vast distance...." Then the exultation passes, and "nothing remains but infinite fatigue and infinite waiting."

*

* *

But I must cut these descriptions short, for I have to consider the leading content of the work, its thought.

In *War and Peace* the profound sense of the destiny which guides mankind is ardently sought, and is found from time to time by the light of some flash of suffering or of genius, found by those few who, through breed or individual sensibility, have exceptional insight: for instance Prince Andrew, Peter Besuhov. But a great roller seems to have passed over the peoples of to-day, reducing all to a level. The most that can happen is that for a moment, now and again, there may rise from the huge flock the isolated bleating of one of the beasts about to die. Thus we have the ethereal figure of Corporal Bertrand, "with his thoughtful smile"—the merest sketch—"a man of few words, never talking of himself"; a man who could once only deliver up the secret of his anguished thoughts—in the twilight hour which follows the killing, just before he himself is killed. He thinks of those whom he has slain in the frenzy of the hand-to-hand fighting:

"It had to be done," he said. "It had to be done, for the sake of the future."

He folded his arms and threw up his head.

"The future!" he cried, all of a sudden. "Those who live after us—what will they think of these killings, ... these exploits, concerning which we who do them do not even know if they are to be compared with those of the heroes of Plutarch and Corneille or with the deeds of apaches!... For all that, mind you, there is one figure that has risen above the war, a figure which will shine with the beauty and the greatness of its courage."

I listened, writes Barbusse, bending towards him, leaning on a stick. I drank in the words that came, in the twilit silence, from lips which rarely broke silence. His voice rang out as he said:

"Liebknecht!"

The same evening, Marthereau, a humble territorial, whose face, bristling with hair, recalled that of a water-spaniel, is listening to a comrade who says: "William is a foul beast, but Napoleon is a great man." This same soldier, after groaning about the war, goes on to speak with delight of the martial ardour displayed by the only son left to him, a boy of five. Marthereau shakes his weary head, his fine eyes shining like those of a puzzled and thoughtful hound. He sighs, saying: "Oh, we're none of us so bad, but we're unlucky, poor devils all of us. But we're too stupid, we're too stupid!"

As a rule, however, the human cry from these lowly fellows is anonymous. We hardly know who has been speaking, for, often enough, all share in a common thought. Born out of common trials, this thought brings them much closer to the other unfortunates in the enemy trenches than to the rest of the world away there in the rear. For visitors from the rear, "trench tourists," for people in the rear, journalists "who exploit the public misery," bellicose intellectuals, the soldiers unite in showing a contempt which is free from violence but knows no bounds. To them has come "the revelation of the great reality": a difference between human beings, a difference far profounder and with far more impassable barriers than those of race: the sharp, glaring, and inalterable distinction, in the population of every country, between those who profit and those who suffer, those who have been compelled to sacrifice everything, those who give to the uttermost of their numbers, of their strength, and of their martyrdom, those over whom the others march forward smiling and successful.

One to whom this revelation has come, says bitterly: "That sort of thing does not encourage one to die!"

But none the less this man meets his death bravely, meekly, like the others.

*

* *

The climax of the work is the last chapter, "The Dawn." It is like an epilogue, the thought in which returns to join the thought in the prologue, "The Vision," but enlarges upon that opening thought, just as in a symphony the promise of the outset is fulfilled at the close.

"The Vision" describes the coming of the declaration of war, shows how the tidings reached a sanatorium in Savoy, facing Mont Blanc. There, these sick men, drawn thither from all the ends of the earth, "detached from the affairs of the world and almost from life itself, ... as remote from their fellow-men as if they already belonged to a future age, look away into the distance, towards the incomprehensible land of the living and the mad." They contemplate the flood below; they watch the shipwrecked nations, grasping at straws. "These thirty millions of slaves, hurled against one another by guilt and by mistake, hurled into war and mud, uplift their human faces whose expression reveals at last a nascent will. The future is in the hands of these slaves, and it is plain that the old world will be transformed by the alliance one day to be made between those whose numbers and whose miseries are infinite."

The concluding chapter, "The Dawn," is a picture of the "flood below," of the lowland inundated by the rain, a picture of the crumbling trenches. The spectacle resembles a scene from the book of Genesis. Germans and French are fleeing together from the scourge of the elements, or are sinking pell-mell into a common grave. Some of these castaways, taking refuge on ridges of mud that stand up amid the waters, begin to awaken from their passivity, and a striking dialogue ensues between the sufferers, like the strophe and antistrophe in a Greek chorus. They are overwhelmed by excess of suffering. Even more are they overwhelmed, "as if by a yet greater disaster," by the thought that in days to come the survivors will be able to forget these ills.

"If only people would remember! If they would only remember, there would be no more wars."

Suddenly, from all sides, rises the cry: "There must never be another war."

Each in turn heaps insults upon war.

"Two armies fighting each other—that's like one great army committing suicide."

One suggests, "It's all right if you win." But the others make answer: "That's no good.—To win settles nothing.—What we need is to kill war."

"Then we shall have to go on fighting after the war?"—"Praps we shall."—"But praps it won't be foreigners we shall be fighting?"—"May be so. The peoples are fighting to-day to get rid of their masters."—"Then one works for the Prussians too?"—"Oh well, we may hope...."—"But we oughtn't to interfere with other folks' business."—"Yes, yes, we ought to, for what you call other folks' business is our own."

"What do people fight for?"—"No one knows what they fight for, but we know whom they fight for. They fight for the pleasure of the few."

The soldiers reckon up these few: "the fighters, those born to power"; those who say, "the races hate one another"; those who say, "I grow fat on the war"; those who say, "there always has been war and there always will be"; those who say, "bow your head, and trust in God"; the sabre-rattlers, the profiteers, the ghouls who batten on the spoils; "the slaves of the past, the traditionalists, for whom an abuse has the force of law because it is of old date."

"Such as these are your enemies quite as much as any of the German soldiers who now share your wretchedness. The German soldiers are no more than poor dupes odiously betrayed and brutalised, domesticated beasts.... But the others are your enemies wherever they were born, whatever the fashion in which they utter their names, and whatever the language in which they lie. Look at them in the heavens above and on the earth beneath! Look at them everywhere! Look well, till you know them, that you may never forget their faces!"

Such is the wail of these armies. But the book closes with a note of hope, with the unspoken oath of international brotherhood, what time a rift forms in the black skies and a calm ray of light falls upon the flooded plain.

*

* *

One ray of sunlight does not make the sky clear, nor is the voice of one soldier the voice of an army. The armies of to-day are nations; and in such armies, as in every nation, there must doubtless conflict and mingle many different currents. Barbusse's story is that of a single squad, almost entirely composed of workers and peasants. But the fact that among these humble folk, among those who, like the third estate in '89, are nothing and shall be all,—that in this proletariat of the armies there is obscurely forming an awareness of universal humanity,—that so bold a voice can be raised from France,—that those who are actually fighting can make a heroic effort to ignore environing wretchedness and imminent death, to dream of the fraternal union of the warring peoples,—I find in this a greatness which surpasses that of all the victories, I find something whose poignant splendour will survive the splendour of battle. I find something which will, I hope, put an end to war.

February, 1917.

"Journal de Genève," March 19, 1917.

XVI

AVE, CÆSAR, MORITURI TE SALUTANT

Dedicated to the Heroic Onlookers in Safe Places.

IN one of the scenes of his terrible and admirable book, *Under Fire,* a record of experiences in the trenches of Picardy, dedicated "To the memory of the comrades who fell by my side at Crouy and on Hill 119," Henri Barbusse depicts two privates going on leave to the neighbouring town. They quit the hell of mud and blood; for months they have been suffering unnamable tortures of body and mind; they now find themselves among comfortable bourgeois who, being at a safe distance from the front, are, of course, bursting with warlike enthusiasm. These carpet-heroes welcome the two men as if they had just returned from a wedding feast. No questions are asked concerning what goes on at the front. The soldiers are told all about it. "It must be splendid, an attack! These masses of men marching forward as to a revel; there's no holding them; they die laughing!" All that our poilus can do is to hold their tongues. One of them says resignedly to his companion: "*They* know more than you do about war and all that goes on at the front. When you get back, if you ever do, with your little bit of truth you will be quite out of it amid that crowd of chatterers."

I do not believe that when the war is over, when all the soldiers have returned home, they will so readily submit to being put in their places by these braggarts of the rear. Already the real fighters are beginning to speak in a singularly bitter and vengeful tone. Barbusse's book bears powerful witness to the fact.

We have other testimonies from the front, less known but no less moving. All of those to which I shall refer have been published. It is my rule, as long as the war lasts, to make no use of personal confidences, oral or written. Things I have been told by friends, known or unknown, are a sacred trust. I shall not use them without special permission, nor until the conditions make it safe. The testimonies I reproduce here have been published in Paris, under a censorship which is extremely strict in the case of the few newspapers that have remained independent. This proves that they describe things that are widely known, things which it is useless or impossible to conceal.

I leave the authors to speak for themselves. Comment is superfluous. The tones are sufficiently clear.

*

* *

Paul Husson, *L'Holocauste* (a collection entitled *Vers et Prose,* published by F. Lacroix, 19 rue de Tournon, Paris, January 10, 1917).—This is the note book of a soldier from the Ile de France. The author "went to the front without enthusiasm, detesting war and devoid of martial ardour. As a soldier he did what all the others did."

p. 19. "In the name of what superior moral principle are these struggles imposed on us? Is it for the triumph of a race? What remains of the glory of Alexander's soldiers or of Cæsar's? To fight, one must have faith. A man must have faith that he is fighting in God's cause, in the cause of some great justice; or else he must love war for its own sake. But we have no faith; we do not love war and we know nothing about it. Yet men fight and die believing neither in the cause of God nor in the great justice; men who do not love war, and who die none the less with their faces to the enemy.... Many, unawakened, go to their deaths without thinking; but others die with anguish in their hearts, anguish at the futile sacrifice and at their realisation of the madness of men."

p. 20. In the trenches. "Everyone was cursing the war, everyone hated it. Some were saying: 'Frenchmen or Germans, they are men like ourselves, they suffer as we do in body and in mind. Do not they, too, dream of the home-coming?' Passing through a village and seeing a man unfit for service because he had lost two fingers, the soldiers had said to him: 'You lucky devil; you needn't go to the war!'"

p. 21. "I am not one of those who believe in the coming of Beauty, Goodness, and Justice.... Nor am I one of those who regild the idols of the past, symbols of obscure forces which it behoves us to worship in silence. I am neither submissive nor a believer.—I love Pity, for we are unfortunates, and it does us good to be solaced, even if we be executioners and butchers. If we do not need consolation for the ills we are suffering, we need consolation for the ills we have done or shall do. We need solace because we have to make others suffer, to kill and be killed."

p. 22. "Lying prone, while the shells whistle overhead, I think. Die! Why should we die on this battlefield?... Die for civilisation, for the freedom of the nations? Words, words, words. We are dying because men are wild beasts killing one another. We are dying for bales of merchandise; we are dying for squabbles about money.—Art, civilisation, and culture are equally beautiful, be they Romance, Teutonic, or Slav. We should love them all!"

p. 59. "With Baudelaire, we detest the weapons of warriors.... The great epoch was the one in which we were living before the war. The flapping of the banners, the long files of soldiers, the roaring of the guns, and the blare of the bugles—these things cannot inspire us with admiration for collective murder and for the monstrous enslavement of the peoples.... Young men lying to-day in your graves, they strew flowers on your tombs and proclaim you immortal. What to you are empty words? They will pass even more quickly than you have passed! It is true that, in any case, within a few years you would have ceased to be. But these few years of life would have been your universe and your strength."

*

* *

André Delemer, *Waiting* (leading article in the fourth issue, dated March, 1917, of the review "Vivre," edited by André Delemer and Marcel Millet, 68 boulevard Rochechouart, Paris).

"If the patriarch of Yasnaya Polyana had been granted a few additional years, superadded to a life already long and full of grief, he would have shuddered before the tragedy of the younger generations. Tolstoi was a man of infinite compassion, and his heart would have been torn with suffering as he contemplated our fate, the fate of those who were suddenly thrust into this colossal war, those who had proclaimed their love for life, those whose faith in the future had seemed an infallible talisman, those who had fervently uttered this great cry of vital affirmation:

"'To live out our youth'—how poignant is the irony of these words; what vistas do they suddenly evoke! All the happiness we have failed to secure, the joys of which we have been deprived, because one evening the order came to us to shoulder our rifles! In twenty years' time people will write about what we have suffered, a suffering which may be compared with the Passion; but we die daily. One galling privilege is ours, that we have lived through a convulsion, that we have been the ransom of past errors and a pledge for the tranquillity of the future. This mission is at once splendid and cruel; simultaneously it exalts and revolts; for the spasm through which we are passing wounds us and immolates us!... To-day the poor quivering refuse raked from the furnace knows all the bitterness of the laurels. Such pride as we retain makes it impossible for us to accept an illusory and transient glory. We know the falsity of attitudinising, and we have probed the emptiness of certain dreams. The fire has licked up the scenery, has reduced the tinsel to ashes. We are now face to face with ourselves, perhaps more fully awakened, certainly more sincere and more disillusioned, for we have secret wounds to heal and great sufferings to lull in the shade! The passing of the days is like wormwood in the mouth.... How painful will be the transition, and how numerous will be the waifs! Already a fresh anguish oppresses our minds; it is this that will afflict when the day comes for the return of those who are still fighting. Terrible will be the anguish as we gaze upon the ruins and the dead encumbering the battlefields! How it will cramp the young wills and annihilate the fine courage of their souls! Troubled and confused epoch, wherein men will be doggedly seeking safer roads and less cruel idols!...

"Young man of my generation, it is you of whom I think as I write these lines, you whom I do not know, though I know that you are still fighting or that you have returned broken from the trenches. I have met you in the street, wearing an almost shamefaced air, doing your best to conceal some infirmity; but in your eyes I have read the intensity of your inward agony. I know the terrible hours through which you have lived, and I know that those who have endured like trials end by having like souls.... I know your doubts; I share your uneasiness. I know how you are obsessed with the question, 'What next?' You, too, are asking what can be seen from the heights, and what is going to happen. I understand your 'What next?'—'To live!' You sing this straight to the hearts of all of us. 'To live!' You embody the cry of our cruel epoch. I have heard this cry, simple yet tremendous, from the lips of the wounded who were aware of the oncoming footsteps of victorious death. I have heard it in the trenches, murmured low like a prayer.—Young man, this is a grievous hour. You are a survivor from the ghastly war; your vitality must affirm itself; you must live. Stripped of all falsehoods, freed from every mirage, you find yourself alone in your nakedness; before you stretches the great white road. Onward, the distance beckons. Leave behind you the old world, and the idols of yesterday. March forward without turning to listen to the outworn voices of the past!"

*

* *

In the name of these young men and their brothers who have been sacrificed in all the lands of the world engaged in mutual slaughter, I throw these cries of pain in the faces of the sacrificers. May the blood sting their faces!

"Revue mensuelle," Geneva, May, 1917.

XVII

AVE, CÆSAR ...

THOSE WHO WISH TO LIVE SALUTE THEE

IN an earlier article I referred to the writings of certain French soldiers. After *Under Fire*, by Henri Barbusse, *L'Holocauste* by Paul Husson and the poignant meditations of André Delemer gave expression to their touching and profoundly human cry. In place of the scandalous idealisations of the war, manufactured far from the front—crude Epinal images, grotesque and false—they give us the stern face of truth, they show us the martyrdom of young men slaughtering one another to gratify the frenzy of criminal elders.

I wish to-day to make known another of these voices, more acerb, more virile, more vengeful, than the stoical bitterness of Husson and the despairing tenderness of Delemer. It is that of our friend Maurice Wullens, editor of "Les Humbles, the literary review of the primary school teachers."

He was severely wounded, and has just been given the war cross with the following honourable mention:

"Wullens (Maurice), soldier of the second class in the eighth company of the seventy-third infantry regiment, a good soldier to whom fear was unknown, dangerously wounded during the defence, against a superior force, of a post which had been entrusted to him."

In "demain," for August, 1917, we find the wonderful story of the fight in which this man was wounded and was then given brotherly help by the German soldiers. As he lay gasping, in expectation of the death-blow, a lad leaned over him smiling, holding out a hand, and saying in German, "Comrade, how do you feel?" And when the wounded man doubted his enemy's sincerity, the latter went on: "Oh, it's all right, comrade! We'll be good comrades! Yes, yes, good comrades." The tale is dedicated:

"To my brother, the anonymous Würtemberg soldier who, in Grurie Wood, on December 30, 1914, withheld his hand when about to slay me, generously saved my life;

"To the (enemy) friend who, in Darmstadt hospital, cared for me like a father;

"And to the comrades E., K., and B., who spoke to me as man to man."

*

* *

This soldier without fear and without reproach, returning to France, discovered there the braggart army of the scribblers at the rear. Their venom and their stupidity infuriated him. But instead of taking refuge, like many of his comrades, in disdainful silence, he did what he had always done, and turned bravely to the attack upon "a superior force." In May, 1916, he became editor of a small magazine, entitled "Les Humbles," but which somewhat belies its name by the ruggedness of its accents and by its refusal to allow its voice to be stifled. He boldly declares:

"Emerged from the whirlwind of the war, but still struggling in its eddies, we do not propose to resign ourselves to the environing mediocrity, to content ourselves with the servile utterance of official platitudes.... We are weary of the daily and systematic stuffing of people's heads with official pabulum.... We have not abdicated any of our rights, not even our hopes."[37]

Each issue of the magazine was a fresh proof of his independence. At this juncture, reviews edited by young thinkers were springing up everywhere from among the ruins. That of Wullens took the leading place, owing to his force of character and his indomitable frankness.

He found a great friend in Han Ryner, who amid the European barbarians, amid the prevailing chaos, exhibits the calm of an exiled Socrates. Gabriel Belot, the engraver, another sage, who, knowing nothing of mental discord or ill-will, dwells on the Ile St. Louis as if the two beautiful arms of the Seine sheltered him from the troubles of the world, lights up the most sombre of articles with the peace of his radiant designs.[38] Other friends, younger men, soldiers like Wullens, rallied to support him in the struggle for the truth. For instance, Marcel Lebarbier, poet and critic.

The most recent issue of "Les Humbles" contains excellent work. Wullens begins with a tribute to the rare French writers who have shown themselves during the last three years to be free-spirited humanists: to Henri Guilbeaux and his periodical "demain";[39] to P. J. Jouve, author of *Vous êtes des hommes* and of *Poème contre le grand crime,* whose sympathetic spirit vibrates and trembles like a tree to the wind of all the pains and all the angers of mankind; to Marcel Martinet, one of the greatest lyricists whom the war (the horror of the war) has brought forth, the writer of *Temps maudits,* a poem which will for ever bear witness to the suffering and the revolt of a free spirit; to Delemer, that moving writer; and to a few recently founded magazines. The editor of "Les Humbles" goes on to clear the ground of what he terms "the false literary vanguard," telling the chauvinist writers what he thinks of them. This lettered poilu, a blunt fellow, does not mince matters:

"I have come from this war whose praises you are singing—I who write.... I have my honourable mention, my war cross: I never wear it. I spent seven months as a war prisoner, before being sent home incapacitated by my wound. I could flood you with war anecdotes. I have no desire to do anything of the kind. Nevertheless I am writing a book on the war. I compress into it all that my heart has felt, all that one man has suffered during these months of unspeakable horror, and likewise all the joy he experienced when he came to perceive, by rare flashes of light, that humanity still lives, that kindliness still exists, on both sides of the Rhine, the world over. You, M. B., sing 'The war in which it is beautiful and sweet to die for our country!' All those who have faced this death will tell you that while it may have been necessary, it was neither beautiful nor sweet.—You glorify the sublime and tattered tricolour: blue is the blouse of our workmen; white is the cornette of our splendid sisters of charity.... You will excuse me for cutting you short before coming to the red, for my unaided memory here suffices me: the red blood of my wounds flowing and clotting on the frozen mud of Argonne that terrible morning in December, 1914; the red mud of pestilential slaughter-houses; the shattered heads of dead comrades; mangled stumps irrigated with peroxide solution so that the living corruption was half hidden by bloodstained foam; red visions glimpsed everywhere in these ghastly and tragical days, you chase one another through the mind tumultuous and hateful. Like the poet, I would fain say, 'A very little more and my heart would break!'"

To bring his philippic to a close he quotes another soldier-author, G. Thuriot-Franchi, who, in the same fighting style, with no pretty phrases and with no concealments, compels these Hectors of the study to swallow their boasts:[40]

"Men who are too young or too old, poets in pyjamas, jealous doubtless of the strategists in slippers, regard it as their duty to be lavish in patriotic song. The trumpets of rhetoric blare; invective has become the chosen method of argument; a thousand blue-stockings, under cover of the Red Cross, when one chats with them out strolling, make a parade of spartan sentiments, amazonian impulses. Whence the plethora of sonnets, odes, stanzas, etc., in which, to speak the jargon of the ordinary critic 'the most exquisite sensibility is happily wedded to the purest patriotism.'—For God's sake leave us alone; you know nothing about it; shut up!"

Thus does a soldier from the front imperiously impose silence upon the false warriors of the rear. If they are fond of the "poilu" style, they will find plenty of it here. Those who have just been looking death in the face have certainly earned the right to speak the plain truth to these "amateurs" of death—the death of others.

"Revue mensuelle," Geneva, October, 1917.

XVIII

MEN IN BATTLE[41]

[*THE MAN OF SORROWS*]

ART is stained with blood. French blood, German blood, it is always the Man of Sorrows. Yesterday we were listening to the sublime and gloomy plaint which breathes from Barbusse's *Under Fire*. To-day come the yet more heartrending accents of *Menschen im Krieg* (Men in Battle). Although they hail from the other camp, I will wager that most of our bellicose readers in France and Navarre will flee from them with stopped ears. For these tones would be a shock to their sensibilities.

Under Fire is more tolerable to these carpet-warriors. There reigns over Barbusse's book a specious impersonality. Despite the multitude and the sharp outline of the figures on his stage, not one of them has a commanding role. We see no hero of romance. Consequently, the reader feels less intimately associated with the hardships recounted on every page; and these hardships, like their causes, have an elemental character. The immensity of the fate which crushes, lessens the agony of those who are crushed. This war fresco resembles the vision of a universal deluge. The human masses execrate the scourge, but accept it passively. *Under Fire* growls forth a threat for the future, but has no menace for the present. Settling-day is postponed until after peace has been signed.

In *Men in Battle*, the court is sitting; mankind is in the witness-box, giving testimony against the butchers. Mankind? Not so. A few men, a few chance victims, whose sufferings, since they are individual, appeal to us more strongly than those of the crowd. We follow the ravages these sufferings make in tortured body and lacerated heart; we wed these sufferings; they become our own. Nor does the witness strain after objectivity. He is the impassioned pleader who, just delivered panting from the rack, cries for vengeance. The writer of the book now under review is newly come from hell; he gasps for breath; his visions chase him; pain's claws have left their mark upon him. Andreas Latzko[42] will, in future days, keep his place in the first rank among the witnesses who have left a truthful record of Man's Passion during 1914, the year of shame.

*

* *

The work is written in the form of six separate stories, united only by a common sentiment of suffering and revolt. There is no logical plan in the arrangement of the six war episodes. The first is entitled "Off to War"; the last, "Home Again." Between, we have "Baptism of Fire," a picture of wounded men; and "A Hero's Death." The centre piece is devoted to "The Victor," the great general, the master of the feast, the responsible and beflattered chief. In the last three stories, physical pain exposes its hideous countenance like that of Medusa mutilated. The two opening stories deal with mental pain. The hero of the centre piece sees neither the one nor the other; his glory is throned on both; he finds life good, and war even better. From the first page to the last, revolt mutters. But on the last page revolt culminates in a murder; a soldier, back from the front, kills a war profiteer.

I give an analysis of the six stories.

"Off to War" (Der Abmarsch) has for its scene the garden of a war hospital in a quiet little Austrian town thirty miles from the front. It is an evening late in autumn. The tattoo has just sounded. All is quiet. From afar comes the sound of heavy guns, as if huge dogs were baying underground. Some young wounded officers are enjoying the peace of the evening. Three of them are talking gaily with two ladies. The fourth, a Landsturm lieutenant, in civil life a well-known composer, sits gloomily apart. He has had a severe nervous shock, and is utterly prostrated, so that not even the arrival of his fair young wife enables him to pull himself together. When she speaks to him, he is unmoved. When she tries to touch him, he draws irritably away. She suffers, and cannot understand his enmity. The other woman takes the lead in the conversation. She is a Frau Major, a major's wife, who spends all her time at the hospital and has acquired there "a peculiar, garrulous cold-bloodedness." She is surfeited with horrors; her endless curiosity gives the impression of hardness and hysterical cruelty. The men are discussing, what is "the finest thing" in the war. According to one of them the finest thing is to find oneself, as this evening, in women's company.

". . . . For five months to see nothing but men—and then all of a sudden to hear a dear woman's clear voice! That's the finest thing of all. It's worth going to war for."

One of the others rejoins that the finest thing is to have a bath, a clean bandage, to get into a nice white bed, to know that for a few weeks you are going to have a rest. Number three says:

"The finest thing of all, I think, is the quiet—when you've been lying up there in the mountains where every shot is echoed five times, and all of a sudden it turns absolutely quiet, no whistling, no howling, no thundering—nothing but a glorious quiet that you can listen to as to a piece of music! The first few nights I sat up the whole time and kept my ears cocked for the quiet, the way you try to catch a tune at a distance. I believe I even shed a tear or two—it was so delightful to listen to no sound."

The three young men tease the last speaker good-naturedly, and they all laugh together. Every one of them is intoxicated by the peace of the sleeping town and the autumn garden. Every one of them wants to make the most of his time, to lose nothing, "to take everything easily with his eyes tight shut, like a child before it enters a dark room."

Now the Frau Major breaks in, breathing more quickly as she speaks:

". . . But, tell me, what was the most awful thing you went through out there?"

The men purse up their lips. This theme does not enter into their program. Suddenly a strident voice speaks out of the darkness:

"Awful? The only awful thing is the going off. You go off to war—and they let you go. That's the awful thing."

A glacial silence follows. The Frau Major makes a bolt for it, to escape hearing the sequel. On the pretext that she has got to get back into the town, and that the last tram is just leaving, she takes with her the unhappy little wife, to whom the husband's words have come as a veiled reproach. The officers are left alone, and one of them, hoping to change the current of thought in the sick man's mind, passes a friendly compliment upon the wife's appearance. The other springs to his feet and says in a fury: "Chic wife? Oh, yes. Very dashing!... She didn't shed a tear when I left on the train. Oh, they were all very dashing when we went off. Poor Dill's wife was, too. Very plucky. She threw roses at him in the train, and she'd been his wife for only two months.... Roses! He, he! 'See you soon again!' They were all so patriotic!..."

He goes on to recount what happened to Dill. Poor Dill was showing to his comrades the new photograph his wife had sent him, when an exploding shell sent a boot flying against his head. In the boot was the leg of a cavalryman who had been blown to pieces many yards away. On the boot was a great spur which stuck into Dill's brain. It took four of them to pull the boot out, and a piece of brain came away with the spur, looking "just like a grey jellyfish." One of the officers, horrified by the tale, rushed away for the doctor. The latter, on arrival, tried to coax the sick man to go in:

"You must go to bed now, Lieutenant...."

"Must go, of course," repeated the lieutenant emphatically, heaving a profound sigh. "We must all go. The man who doesn't go is a coward, and they have no use for a coward. That's how it is. Don't you understand? Heroes are in fashion now. The chic Madame Dill wanted a hero to match her new hat. Ha, ha! That's why poor Dill had to have his brains spilled. I must go; you must go; we must all go to die.... The women look on, plucky, because that's the fashion now...."

He gazed round questioningly.

"Isn't it sad?" he asked softly. Then, in a fury once more, he cried:

"Weren't they humbugging us?... Was I an assassin? Was I a swashbuckler? Didn't I suit her when I sat at the piano playing? We were expected to be gentle and considerate! Considerate! And all at once, because the fashion changed, they wanted us to be murderers. Do you understand? Murderers!"

Speaking now in a lower tone, he went on plaintively:

"My wife was in the fashion too, of course. Not a tear! I kept waiting, waiting for her to begin to weep, to beg me to get out of the train, not to go with the others—beg me to be a coward for her sake. But none of them had the pluck to do that. They all wanted to be in the fashion. Mine too! Mine too! She waved her handkerchief, just like the others."

His twitching arms writhed upwards, as though he were calling the heavens to witness.

"You want to know what was the most awful thing? The disillusionment was the most awful thing—the going off. The war wasn't. The war is what it has to be. Did it surprise you to find out that war is horrible? The only surprising thing was the going off. To find out that women are cruel—that was the surprising thing. That they can smile and throw roses; that they can give up their husbands, their children, the little boys they have put to bed a thousand times, tucked up a thousand times, have fondled, have created from their own flesh and blood. That was the surprise. That they gave us up—that they sent us—actually sent us. For every one of them would have been ashamed to stand there without a hero. That was the great disillusionment.... Do you think we should have gone if they had not sent us? Do you think so?... No general could have done anything if the women hadn't allowed us to be packed into the trains, if they had screamed out that they would never look at us again if we became murderers. Not a man would have gone if they had sworn never to give themselves to one who had split open other men's skulls or shot and bayoneted his fellows. Not one man, I tell you, would have gone. I didn't want to believe that they could stand it like that. 'They're only pretending,' I thought. 'They're just holding themselves in. But when the whistle blows they'll begin to scream, and tear us out of the train, and rescue us.' That one time they had the chance to protect us. But all they cared about was to be in the fashion!..."

He broke down, and collapsed once more on to the bench. He began to weep. A little circle of people had formed round him. The doctor said gently:

"Come, come, Lieutenant, let's get along to bed. Women are like that, you know, and we can't help it."

The sick man leapt to his feet in a rage.

"Women are like that? Women are like that? Since when? Since when? Have you never heard of the suffragettes who boxed the ears of ministers of state, who set museums on fire, who chained themselves to lamp-posts, all for the sake of the vote? For the sake of the vote, do you hear? But for the sake of their men? Nothing!"

He paused to take breath, overwhelmed with a throttling despair. Then, fighting with sobs, like a hunted beast, he cried out:

"Have you heard of one woman throwing herself in front of the train for the sake of her husband? Has a single one of them slapped a statesman's face, or tied herself to the railway lines, for our sake? Not one has had to be saved from such desperate courses.... The whole world over, not one of them has moved a finger for us. They drove us forth! They gagged us! They gave us the spur, like poor Dill. They sent us to murder, they sent us to die—for their vanity. Are you going to defend them? No! They must be plucked out. Like weeds, they must be torn up by the roots! You must pull four at a time, as we had to do with Dill. Four of you together, then you'll get her up. Are you the doctor? There! Do it to my head! I don't want a wife! Pull—pull her out!"

He struck himself on the head with his fist. He was dragged into the house, howling at the top of his voice. Soon the garden was empty. By degrees the lights were extinguished and the noise was stilled, except for the distant artillery fire. The patrol which had helped to take the madman back into the hospital repassed, with the old corporal in the rear, hanging his head. From afar off came the flash of an explosion, followed by a prolonged rumbling. The old man stood still, listened, shook his fist, spat disgustedly, and muttered:

"Oh, Hell!"

I have given lengthy extracts from this story, for I wished to convey a notion of the author's pulsating, vibrant, and impassioned style. There is more of the drama here than of the novel, and an elemental fierceness like that of Shakespearean drama. It would be well if these pages, so profound in the bitterness of their injustice, were to become widely known. It would be well if the poor women who, in all love as a rule, adopt a superhuman pose, could be made to realise, by means of this madman's outpourings, the secret thoughts which no man will dare to tell them, to understand the mute and almost shamefaced appeal to their poor human kindliness, to their simple and motherly compassion.

*

* *

I shall deal more briefly with the other episodes.

The second, "Baptism of Fire" (Feuertaufe), is long, perhaps too long, but full of pity and of pain. Almost the whole scene is played within the soul of Captain Marschner, a man of fifty, who is leading his company to the front-line trench under the enemy's fire. He is not a professional soldier. As a young man he had been an officer, but at the age of thirty he had gone to school again, wishing to quit the trade of war and to become a civil engineer. Now the war had brought him back to the army. He had been in Vienna only the day before yesterday. His men were fathers of families, stonemasons, peasants, factory hands, and so on. None of them had any patriotic enthusiasm. He read their minds, and felt ashamed of himself because he was leading to certain death these poor fellows who trusted him. Beside him marched Weixler, a young lieutenant, cold, ruthless, inhuman—as one so often is at twenty years of age "when one has had no time yet to learn the value of life." The hardness of this man (an irreproachable officer) arouses in Marschner mingled anger and suffering. By degrees a fierce but unspoken feud arises between them. At the very end, just when open war is about to break out between the two, a huge shell bursts in their trench and both are buried under the wreckage. The captain comes to himself with a shattered skull. At a few paces' distance lies the implacable lieutenant, his entrails trailing on the ground beside him. They exchange a last look. Marschner sees a face that is almost strange to him, pale and sad, with timid eyes. The whole expression is gentle and plaintive; there is an unforgettable air of tender, anxious resignation.

"He is suffering!" flashed through the captain's mind. "He is suffering!" Marschner is transported with joy. And therewith he dies.

"My Comrade" (Der Kamarad) is the diary of a soldier in hospital. This man has been driven mad by the terrible sights at the front, and above all by the vision of a wounded man in the death agony, a poor wretch whose face had been torn away by a grapnel. The sight was seared upon his brain. The image never left him by day or by night. It sat down beside him at meals; went to bed with him; got up with him in the morning. It had become "My Comrade." The description is positively hallucinating, and this story contains some of the most forceful passages in the book, directed against the warmongers and against the humbugs of the press.

"A Hero's Death" (Heldentod) describes the death in hospital of First Lieutenant Otto Kadar. He has a fractured skull. While the regimental officers were listening to a gramophone playing the Rakoczy march, a bomb exploded among them. The dying man never stops talking of the Rakoczy march. He imagines that he is looking at the corpse of a young officer whose head has been carried away, and in place of the head, screwed into the neck, is the gramophone disc. In his growing delirium, he fancies that the same thing has happened to all the common soldiers, to all the officers, to himself; that in each one the head has been replaced by a gramophone disc. That is why it is so easy to lead them to the slaughter. The dying man makes a frantic effort to tear away the disc from his own neck, and as he does so all is over. The old major looking on says in a voice vibrating with respect: "He died like a true Hungarian—singing the Rakoczy march."

"Home Again" (Heimkehr) tells of the homecoming of Johann Bogdan, who had been the handsomest man in his native village. He returns from the war hopelessly disfigured. In hospital his face has been remade for him by means of a number of plastic operations. But when he looks at himself in the glass he is horror-stricken. No one in the village recognises him. The only exception is a hunchback whom he had looked on with contempt, and who now greets him familiarly. The countryside has been transformed by the building of a munition factory. Marcsa, Bogdan's betrothed, works there, and has become the factory owner's mistress. Bogdan sees red, and stabs the man, to be struck down dead himself a moment later.—In this story the growth of the revolutionary spirit is manifest. Bogdan, a dull conservative by nature, is inspired with it against his will. We have a threatening vision of the return of the soldiers from all the armies, and of how they will take vengeance upon those who sent others to death while remaining at home to enjoy life and to grow rich by speculation.

I have kept the third story to the last, for it contrasts with the others by the sobriety of its emotion. It is entitled "The Victor" (Der Sieger).

In the other episodes, the tragic element is nude and bleeding. Here tragedy is veiled with irony, and is all the more formidable. Revolt simmers beneath the calm words; the butchers are pilloried by the bitter satire.

The victor is His Excellency the Commander-in-Chief, the renowned Generalissimo X., universally known in the press as "The Victor of * * *." He is there in all his glory, in the principal square of the town which is now the military headquarters. Here he is absolute master. Here there is nothing which he cannot do or undo at his will. The band is playing, on a fine autumn afternoon. His Excellency sits out of doors in front of a café, amid smart officers and elegantly dressed ladies. It is nearly forty miles from the front. Strict orders have been given that no wounded or convalescent soldier, or any man whose appearance might have a depressing effect on the general war enthusiasm or might trouble the comfort of those who are at ease, shall be allowed out of hospital. We are told how much His Excellency is enjoying himself. He finds the war splendid. People have never had a jollier time. "Did you notice the young fellows back from the front? Sunburnt, healthy, happy!... I assure you the world has never been so healthy as it is now." The whole company chimes in to celebrate the beneficial effects of the war. His Excellency meditates upon his good luck, his titles, his decorations, harvested in a single year of war, after he had vegetated for nine-and-thirty years in peace and mediocrity. It has been a perfect miracle. He is now a national hero. He has his motor, his country mansion, his chef, delicate fare, a lordly retinue of servants—and he has not to pay a penny for it. Only one thing troubles his reflections, the thought that the whole fairy tale may vanish as suddenly as it came, and that he may relapse into obscurity. What if the enemy were to break through? But he reassures himself. All is going well. The great enemy offensive, which has been expected for the last three months, and which actually began twenty-four hours ago, hurls itself vainly against a wall of iron. "The human reservoir is full to overflowing. Two hundred thousand young stalwarts of exactly the right age are ready to be caught up in the whirl of the dance, until they sink in a marish of blood and bones." His Excellency's agreeable reverie is interrupted by an aide-de-camp, who informs him that the correspondent of an influential foreign newspaper has requested an interview. This scene is brilliantly described. The general does not allow the journalist to get a word in. He has his speech ready:

"He delivered it now, speaking with emphasis, and pausing occasionally to recall what came next. First of all, he referred to his gallant soldiers, lauding their courage, their contempt for death, their doings glorious beyond description. He went on to express regret that it was impossible to reward all these heroes according to their deserts. Raising his voice, he invoked the fatherland's eternal gratitude for such loyalty and self-renunciation even unto death. Pointing to the heavy crop of medals on his chest, he explained that the distinctions conferred on him were really a tribute to his men. Finally he interwove a few well-chosen remarks anent the military calibre of the enemy and the skilled generalship displayed by the other side. His last words conveyed his inviolable confidence in ultimate victory."

When the oration was finished, the general became the man of the world.

"You are going to the front now?" he asked with a courteous smile, and responded to the journalist's enthusiastic "yes" with a melancholy sigh.

"Lucky man! I envy you. You see, the tragedy in the life of the modern general is that he cannot lead his men personally into the fray. He spends his whole life making ready for war; he is a soldier in body and mind, and yet he knows the excitement of battle only from hearsay."

Of course the correspondent is delighted that he will be able to depict this all-powerful warrior in the sympathetic role of renunciation.

The agreeable scene is disturbed by the intrusion of an infantry captain who is out of his mind and has escaped from hospital. His Excellency, though in a towering rage, controls his temper for the sake of appearances, and has the inconvenient visitor sent back in his own car. He turns the incident to account by uttering a few touching phrases concerning the impossibility for a general to do his duty if he had to witness all the misery at the front. He evades the correspondent's final question, "When does Your Excellency hope for peace?" by pointing across the square to the old cathedral, saying, "The only advice I can give you is to go over there and ask our Heavenly Father. No one else can answer that question."—Then His Excellency descends upon the hospital like a whirlwind, blusters at the old staff-surgeon, and reiterates the order to keep all the patients safely under lock and key. His wrath by now is slightly assuaged, but it is revived by a message from the front. A brigadier-general reports terrible losses, and declares that he cannot hold the line without reinforcements. It was part of His Excellency's plan that this brigade should be wiped out, after resisting the attack as long as possible. But he is angry that his victims should have any advice to offer, and sends curt orders, "The sector is to be held."—At length, the day's work being over, the great man drives home in his motor, still fiercely excogitating the correspondent's idiotic question, "When does Your Excellency hope for peace?"

"Hope!... How tactless!... Hope for peace! What good has a general to expect from peace? Could not this civilian understand that a commander-in-chief is only a commander-in-chief in war-time, and that in peace-time he is nothing more than a professor with a collar of gold braid?"

The general is annoyed once more when the car pulls up because it is necessary to close the hood on account of the rain. But during the pause His Excellency hears the sound of distant firing. His eyes brighten.—Thank God, there was still war.

*

* *

My quotations have been enough to show the emotional force and the trenchant irony of Latzko's book. It scorches. It is a torch of suffering and revolt. Both its merits and its defects are sib to this frenzy. The author is master of the writer's art, but he is not always master of his own feelings. His memories are still open wounds. He is possessed by his visions. His nerves vibrate like violin strings. Almost without exception, his analyses of emotion are tremulous monologues. His shattered spirit cannot find repose.

Doubtless he will be criticised for the preponderant place assumed in his book by physical pain. The work is full of it. Pain monopolises the reader's mind and wearies his eyes. Not until we have read *Men in Battle* do we fully appreciate Barbusse's chariness in the use of material effects. If Latzko is persistent in their employment, this is not merely because he is haunted by memories of pain. He wishes, deliberately wishes, to communicate these impressions to others, for he has suffered greatly from others' insensibility.

In very truth, such insensibility has been the saddest of all our experiences during this war. We knew man to be stupid, mediocre, selfish: we knew that on occasions man could be extremely cruel. But though we had few illusions, we had never believed that man could remain so monstrously indifferent to the cries of millions of victims. We had never believed that there could be a smile such as we have witnessed upon the lips of the young fanatics and of the old demoniacs who, from their safe seats, are never weary of looking on at the mutual slaughter of the nations, of those who kill one another for the pleasure, the pride, the ideas, and the interests of the onlookers. All the rest, all the crimes, we can tolerate; but this aridity of soul is the worst of all, and we feel that Latzko has been overwhelmed by it. Like one of his own characters, who is regarded as a sick man because he cannot forget the sufferings he has witnessed, Latzko cries to the apathetic public:

"Sick!... No! It is the others that are sick. They are sick who gloat over news of victories and see conquered miles of territory arise resplendent above mountains of corpses. They are sick who stretch a barrier of many-coloured bunting between themselves and their better feelings, lest they should see what crimes are being committed against their brothers in the beyond that they call 'the front.' Every man is sick who can still think, talk, argue, sleep, knowing that other men, holding their own entrails in their hands, are crawling like half-crushed worms across the furrows in the fields, and are dying like animals before they can reach the ambulance station, while somewhere, far away, a woman with longing in her heart is dreaming beside an empty bed. All those are sick who fail to hear the moaning, the gnashing of teeth, the howling, the crashing and bursting, the wailing and cursing and agonising in death, because their ears are filled with the murmur of everyday affairs. These blind and deaf ones are sick, not I. Sick are those dumb beings whose soul can give voice neither to compassion nor to anger...." ("My Comrade").

The author's aim is to arouse these sick beings from their torpor, to treat them with the actual cautery of pain. This aim is portrayed in the person of Captain Marschner ("Baptism of Fire"), who, when his company is in the thick of the slaughter, suffers from nothing so intensely as from the harsh impassivity of his lieutenant, but who, himself at the point of death, finds it a positive solace to see on Weixler's stern face a shadow of pain, brotherly pain.

"Thank God," he thinks. "At last he knows what suffering is!"

"Through sympathy to knowledge," sings the mystical chorus of *Parsifal*.

This "suffering with others" (sympathy, Mitleid), this "pain which unites," overflows from the work of Andreas Latzko.

November 15, 1917.

"Les Tablettes," Geneva, December, 1917.

XIX

VOX CLAMANTIS....[43]

AFTER the glacial torpor of the early days of the war, mutilated art begins to bloom anew. The irrepressible song of the soul wells up out of suffering. Man is not merely, as he is apt to boast, a reasoning animal (he might, with better ground, term himself an unreasoning one); he is a singing animal; he can no more get on without singing than without bread. We learn it amid the very trials through which we are passing to-day. Although the general suppression of liberty in Europe has doubtless deprived us of the deeper music, of the most intimate confessions, we nevertheless hear great voices rising from every land. Some of these, coming from the armies, sing in sad and epic strains. See, for example, *Under Fire* by Henri Barbusse, and the heart-rending tales issued by Andreas Latzko under the collective title of *Men in Battle*. Others express the pain and horror of those who, remaining at home, look on at the butchery without taking part in it, and who, being inactive, suffer all the more from the torments of thought. To this category belong the impassioned poems of Marcel Martinet[44] and P. J. Jouve.[45] Paying less attention to suffering and more concerned with understanding, the English novelists, H. G. Wells[46] and Douglas Goldring,[47] give a faithful analysis of the distressing errors amid which they move and which they themselves by no means escape. Yet others, finally, taking refuge in the contemplation of the past, rediscover there the same circle of misfortunes and of hopes—rediscover the "eternal cycle." They cloak their grief in the fashions of other days, thus ennobling it and despoiling it of its poisoned dart. From the lofty eyrie of the ages, set free by art, the soul contemplates suffering as in a vision, no longer aware whether that suffering belongs to the present or to the past. Stefan Zweig's *Jeremias* is the finest contemporary specimen known to me of this august melancholy which, looking beyond the bloody drama of to-day, is able to see in it the eternal tragedy of mankind.

Not without struggle can such serene regions be attained. A friend of Zweig before the war, his friend to-day, I have witnessed all that was endured by this free European spirit whom the war robbed of that which he had held most dear; robbed him of his artistic and humanist faith, thereby depriving him of any reason for existence. The letters he wrote me during the first year of the war reveal his agonising torments in all their tragical beauty. By degrees, however, the immensity of the catastrophe, communion with the universal sorrow, restored to him the calm which resigns itself to destiny; for he came to see that destiny leads to God, who is the union of souls. Of the Hebrew race, he has drawn his inspiration from the Bible. It was easy to find there analogous instances of national madness, of the fall of empires, and of heroic patience. One figure, above all, attracted him, that of the great forerunner, Jeremiah the persecuted prophet, foretelling the woeful peace which was to flourish upon the ruins.

Zweig devotes to Jeremiah a dramatic poem, which I propose to analyse, making extensive quotations. The work consists of nine scenes. It is written in prose mingled with verse, sometimes free, sometimes rhymed, the transition from prose to verse occurring when emotion breaks from control. The form is ample and rhetorical. There is a majestic balance in the exposition of the thought; but the poem would perhaps have been better for condensation, for this would have left more to the reader's imagination. The common people play a leading part in the action. Their sallies and counter-sallies jostle one another; but at the close their voices unite in measured choruses, breathing the thoughts of the prophet, the guardian of Israel. Zweig has steered his course skilfully between the dangers of archaism and anachronism. We rediscover our preoccupations of the moment in this epic of the fall of Jerusalem; but we find them as the faithful of recent centuries found day by day in their Bible the light which lightened their road in hours of difficulty—sub specie aeternitatis.

"Jeremiah is our prophet," Stefan Zweig said to me. "He has spoken for us, for our Europe. The other prophets came at their due time. Moses spoke and acted. Jesus died and acted. Jeremiah spoke in vain. His people failed to understand him. The times were not ripe. He could only prophesy, and bewail the approaching doom. He could do nothing to prevent what was to happen. Ours is a like fate."

But there are defeats more fruitful than victories; there are griefs more illuminating than joys. Zweig's poem shows this magnificently. At the end of the drama, Israel has been crushed. The Jews, leaving their ruined city, going into exile, pass towards the future filled with an inward radiance never known to them before, strong by reason of the sacrifices which have revealed to them their mission.

*

* *

SCENE ONE

THE PROPHET'S AWAKENING.

A night in early spring. All is quiet. Jeremiah, awakened with a start by a vision of Jerusalem in flames, goes up to the terrace which overlooks his dwelling and the town. He is "poisoned" by dreams, obsessed by the oncoming storm, although peace still broods over the scene. He does not understand the fierce energy which surges up in him; but he knows that it comes from God and he awaits his orders, uneasy and under the spell of hallucination. His mother calls to him, and at first he imagines her voice to be the voice of God. To the terrified woman he foretells the ruin of Jerusalem. She implores him to be silent; his words seem to her sacrilegious and arouse her anger; to close his mouth, she tells him he will have her curse if he makes his sinister dreams known to others. But Jeremiah is no longer his own man. He follows the unseen Master.

SCENE TWO

THE WARNING.

In the great square of Jerusalem, in front of the temple and the king's palace, the people acclaim the Egyptian envoys who have brought with them a daughter of the Pharaoh to wed King Zedekiah, and who are to cement an alliance against the Chaldeans. Abimelech the general, Pashur the high priest, Hananiah the official prophet who prophesies falsely in order to inflame the passion of the people, incite the crowd to frenzy. Young Baruch is one of the most violent among those who clamour for war. Jeremiah resists the stream of fury. He condemns the war. He is immediately charged with having been bought by Chaldean gold. Hananiah, the false prophet, sings the praises of "the holy war, the war of God."

JEREMIAH. Do not bring God's name into the war. Men make war, not God. No war is holy; no death is holy; life alone is holy.

BARUCH. Thou liest, thou liest! Life is given us solely that we may sacrifice it to God.

The crowd is carried away by the hope of an easy victory. A woman spits upon Jeremiah the pacifist. Jeremiah curses her.

JEREMIAH. Cursed be the man who thirsts for blood! But seven times cursed be the woman who thirsts for war. War will devour the fruit of her body.

His violence is terrifying. He is charged to hold his peace. He refuses, for Jerusalem is within him, and Jerusalem does not wish to die.

JEREMIAH. The walls of Jerusalem stand erect in my heart, and they do not wish to fall.... Safeguard peace!

The fickle crowd, despite itself, is being swayed by his words, when General Abimelech returns in a fury. He has just left the king's council, where a majority has voted against the alliance with Egypt. In his wrath, he has thrown away his sword. Young Israel, through the voice of Baruch, acclaims him as a national hero. The high priest blesses him. Hananiah, prophet and demagogue, fires the crowd to flock to the palace that they may force the king to declare war. Jeremiah tries to stop the yelling mob. He is knocked down. Young Baruch strikes him with a sword. The crowd passes on.

But Baruch, appalled, stays with his victim, staunches the blood which flows from the wound, and begs for pardon. Jeremiah, helped to his feet, thinks only of rejoining the maddened crowd, to cry his message of peace. This inviolable energy astounds Baruch, who had regarded as a coward anyone who should condemn action or preach peace.

JEREMIAH. Dost thou imagine that peace is not action, that peace is not the action of all actions? Day by day thou shouldst wrest it from the mouth of the liars and from the heart of the crowd. Thou shouldst stand alone against all.... Those who desire peace are for ever fighting.

Baruch is overcome.

BARUCH. I believe in thee, for I have seen thy blood poured forth for thy words.

Jeremiah vainly endeavours to dissuade him. The prophet is unwilling that Baruch should share in his dreams and his awesome fate. But Baruch insists upon joining Jeremiah, and the young man's ardent faith is superadded to and redoubles that of the prophet.

JEREMIAH. Thou believest in me when I myself scarcely believe in my own dreams.... Thou hast made my blood flow and hast mingled thy will with mine.... Thou art the first to believe in me, the first-born of my faith, the son of my anguish.

The crowd flocks back into the square, uttering cries of delight, for war has been decided on. Heading a solemn procession, the king appears, gloomy, with naked sword. Hananiah dances before him, like David. Jeremiah cries out to the king, "Throw down the sword. Save Jerusalem! Peace! God's peace!" His words are drowned by the shouting, and he is pushed aside. But the king has heard. He halts for a moment, looking round and trying to find the speaker. Then, sword in hand, he marches forward, and goes up into the temple.

SCENE THREE

RUMOURS.

The war has begun. The crowd is awaiting news. They talk at random, catching at the words which please them, or shaping utterances which express their wishes. Longing for victory, they imagine it won. In masterly fashion, Zweig shows how a vague rumour spreads in the hallucinated mind of the multitude, to attain in an instant a certainty surpassing that of truth. Details pass from mouth to mouth; precise figures of the false victory are given. Jeremiah, the defeatist prophet, is mocked. The bird of ill-omen is informed that the Chaldeans have been crushed, and that King Nebuchadnezzar has been slain. Jeremiah, at first dumb with astonishment, thanks God for having turned to derision his gloomy forebodings. Then, pricked by the foolish pride of the people, who become brutishly intoxicated with the victory and have learned nothing from their trials, he scourges them with new threats.

JEREMIAH. Your joy will be brief.... God will rend it asunder like a curtain.... Already the messenger is afoot, the bearer of evil tidings, he is running, he is running; his swift footsteps lead towards Jerusalem. Already, already, he is at hand, the messenger of fear, the messenger of terror, already the messenger is at hand.

And lo, the messenger enters, panting for breath. Before he speaks, Jeremiah trembles with fear.

MESSENGER. The enemy is victorious. The Egyptians have come to terms with the Chaldeans. Nebuchadnezzar is marching on Jerusalem.

The crowd utters cries of terror. In the king's name a herald issues the call to arms. Jeremiah, the seer whose visions have been too faithfully fulfilled, Jeremiah from whose neighbourhood the panic-stricken folk withdraw, vainly implores God to convict him of falsehood.

SCENE FOUR

THE WATCH ON THE RAMPARTS.

Moonlight. On the walls of Jerusalem. The enemy is at work. In the distance Samaria and Gilgal are seen in flames. Two sentinels are conversing. One, a professional soldier, neither can nor will see anything beyond his orders. The other, who seems one of our brothers of to-day, is trying to understand, and his heart is racked.

SECOND SOLDIER. Why does God hurl the nations against one another? Is there not room for all beneath the heavens? What are nations?... What puts death between the nations? What is it which sows hatred when there is room and to spare for life, and when there is abundance of scope for love? I can't understand, I can't understand.... This crime cannot be God's will. He has given us our lives that we may live them.... War does not come from God. Whence comes it then?

He thinks that if he could talk matters over with a Chaldean, they would come to an understanding. Why should not they talk things over? He would like to summon one, to hold out a friendly hand. The other soldier grows angry.

FIRST SOLDIER. You shall not do that. They are our enemies, and it is our duty to hate them.

SECOND SOLDIER. Why should I hate them if my heart knows no reason for hatred?

FIRST SOLDIER. They began the war; they were the aggressors.

SECOND SOLDIER. Yes, that is what we say in Jerusalem. In Babylon, perchance, they use the same words of us. If we could talk things over with them, we might get some light on the question.... Whom do we serve by compassing their death?

FIRST SOLDIER. We serve God and the king our master.

SECOND SOLDIER. But God said, and it is written, Thou shalt not kill.

FIRST SOLDIER. It is likewise written, An eye for an eye and a tooth for a tooth.

SECOND SOLDIER (sighs). Many things are written. Who can understand them all?

He continues to bewail himself aloud. The first soldier urges him to be silent.

SECOND SOLDIER. How can a man help questioning himself, how can he be other than uneasy, at such an hour? Do I know where I am and how long I have still to stand on guard?... How can I fail, while I live, to question the meaning of life?... Maybe death is already within me; perchance the questioner is no longer life, but death.

FIRST SOLDIER. You are only tormenting yourself about nothings.

SECOND SOLDIER. God has given us a heart precisely that it may torment us.

Jeremiah and Baruch appear on the ramparts. Jeremiah leans over the parapet and gazes down. All that he is now looking at, these fires, these myriad tents, this first night of the siege, are things with which he is already familiar from his visions. There is not a star in heaven which he has not seen in this place. He can no longer deny that God has chosen him. He must give his message to the king, for he knows the end; he sees it; he describes it in prophetic verses.

King Zedekiah, full of fear, making his rounds with Abimelech, hears the voice of Jeremiah, and recognises it as the voice of the one who wished to hold him back on the threshold of the declaration of war. He would pay heed now, could the decision be made over again. Jeremiah assures him that it is never too late to ask peace. Zedekiah is unwilling to be the first to move. What if his proposals were rejected?

JEREMIAH. Happy are they who are rejected for justice' sake.

But what if people laugh at him? asks Zedekiah.

JEREMIAH. It is better to be followed by the laughter of fools than by the tears of widows.

Zedekiah refuses. He would rather die than humble himself. Jeremiah curses him and calls him the murderer of his people. The soldiers wish to throw him from the wall. Zedekiah restrains them. His calm, his forbearance, perplex Jeremiah, who lets the king depart without making any further effort to save him. The decisive moment has been lost. Jeremiah accuses himself of weakness; he feels himself impotent, and he despairs; he knows only how to cry aloud and to utter curses. He does not know how to do good. Baruch consoles him. At Jeremiah's suggestion, Baruch decides to climb down the walls into the Chaldean camp, that he may parley with Nebuchadnezzar.

SCENE FIVE

THE PROPHET'S ORDEAL.

Jeremiah's mother is dying. The sick woman knows nothing of what is happening outside. Since she drove her son from home she has been suffering and waiting. Both mother and son are proud, and neither will make the first advance. Ahab, the old servitor, has taken it upon himself to fetch Jeremiah. The sick woman awakens and calls her son. He appears, but dares not draw near, because of the curse which weighs on him. His mother stretches out her arms. They embrace one another. In affectionate dialogue, versified, they recount their love and their grief. The mother rejoices at seeing her son once more. She believes him to be convinced that he was mistaken in the past, that his visions were false. "I was certain," says she, "that the enemy would never, never besiege Jerusalem." Jeremiah cannot hide his uneasiness. She notices it, grows uneasy herself, asks questions, guesses, "There is war in Israel!" Panic seizes her; she tries to leave her bed. Jeremiah endeavours to quiet her. She begs him to swear that there is no enemy, no danger. The attendants whisper to Jeremiah, "Swear! swear!" Jeremiah cannot lie. The mother dies terror-stricken. Hardly has she breathed her last when Jeremiah swears the falsehood. But the oath comes too late. The enraged witnesses chase forth the unfeeling son who has killed his mother. An angry crowd wishes to stone him. The high priest has him thrown into prison, to gag his prophecies. Jeremiah accepts the sentence unrepiningly. He wishes to live under shadow of night, he is eager to be delivered from this world, to be brother of the dead.

SCENE SIX

MIDNIGHT VOICES.

The king's room. Zedekiah, at the window, is looking out over the moonlit town. He envies other kings, who can hold counsel with their gods, or who can learn the will of the gods from soothsayers. "It is terrible to be the servant of a God who is always silent; whom no one has ever seen." The king has to advise others; but who will advise the king?

Nevertheless, here are his five closest counsellors, whom he has summoned to his presence: Pashur the high priest; Hananiah the prophet; Imri the elder; Abimelech the general; Nahum the steward. For eleven months Jerusalem has been besieged. No help is coming. What is to be done? All agree that it is essential to hold out. Nahum alone is gloomy; there remains food for three weeks only. Zedekiah asks their opinion concerning the opening of negotiations with Nebuchadnezzar. They are opposed to it, save Imri and Nahum. The king tells them that an envoy from Nebuchadnezzar has already come. He is summoned. Baruch is the envoy. He states the terms of the Chaldeans. Nebuchadnezzar, admiring the courageous resistance of the Jews, agrees to spare their lives if they open their gates. All that he demands is the humiliation of Zedekiah, who was king by his grace and who shall be king once more, by Nebuchadnezzar's grace, when his fault has been atoned. Let Zedekiah abase himself before the victor, yoke on neck and crown in hand! Zedekiah is indignant, and Abimelech supports his objection. But the others, who think that the Jews are getting off cheaply, explain to the king how splendid will be his sacrifice. Zedekiah, overborne, agrees; he will resign the crown to his son.—But Nebuchadnezzar has additional demands. He wishes to look upon the One who is Master in Israel; he wishes to enter the temple. Pashur and Hananiah are outraged by this sacrilegious suggestion. The matter is put to the vote. Abimelech abstains, saying that his business is to act, not to discuss. The others are two for and two against. It devolves on the king to give the casting vote. He tells the advisers to leave him to himself that he may think the matter over. He is on the point of constraining himself to accept the Chaldeans' terms, when Baruch admits that the visit to Nebuchadnezzar to sue for peace was made at Jeremiah's instigation. Zedekiah is enraged at this name which he thought he had heard the last of. He has immured Jeremiah's body, but the prophet's thought continues to act, and to cry "Peace!" The king's pride is wounded, and he refuses to yield to the ascendancy of the prophet. He despatches Baruch to the Chaldeans with an insulting answer. But hardly has Baruch departed, when Zedekiah regrets his precipitancy. He vainly tries to sleep. Jeremiah's voice fills his thoughts, seems to break the silence of the night. Sending for the prophet, the king quietly recounts Nebuchadnezzar's terms, but does not say that they have been refused. He endeavours to secure Jeremiah's approval for the course he has chosen, hoping thus to appease his conscience. But the prophet reads his hidden thoughts, and utters lamentations upon Jerusalem. Soon, seized with frenzy, Jeremiah portrays the destruction of the city. He foretells Zedekiah's punishment; the king's eyes will be put out after he has witnessed the death of his three sons. Zedekiah, furious at first and then quailing, throws himself on his bed, weeping, and pleading for mercy. Jeremiah goes on unheeding, down to the final curse. Then he awakens from his trance, no less shattered than his victim. Zedekiah, no longer angry, no longer in revolt, recognises the prophet's power; he believes in Jeremiah, believes in the terrible predictions.

ZEDEKIAH. Jeremiah, I did not want war. I was forced to declare war, but I loved peace. And I loved thee because of thy love for peace.

Not with a light heart did I take up arms.... I have suffered greatly, as thou canst testify when the time comes. Be thou near me if thy words are fulfilled.

JEREMIAH. I shall be near thee, Zedekiah my brother. The prophet is leaving, when the king recalls him.

ZEDEKIAH. Death is upon me, and I see thee for the last time. Thou hast cursed me, Jeremiah. Bless me, now, ere we part.

JEREMIAH. The Lord bless thee, and keep thee in all thy ways. May the light of His countenance shine upon thee, and may He give thee peace.

ZEDEKIAH (as in a dream). May He give us peace.

SCENE SEVEN

THE SUPREME AFFLICTION.

The following morning, in the great square before the temple. The famished crowd clamours for bread, prepares to attack the palace, threatens Nahum the forestaller. Abimelech, to rescue him, sends soldiers to the attack. Amid the riot, a voice is heard crying that the enemy has forced one of the gates. The people utter wails of terror, cursing king, priests, and prophets. Their thoughts fly to Jeremiah, who alone foretold the truth. He is their only hope. They break into his prison, and bring him forth, in triumph, shouting: "Saint! Master! Samuel! Elijah!... Save us!"—Jeremiah, heavy-hearted, does not at first understand. When he hears them accuse the king of having sold the people, he exclaims, "It is false!"

THE CROWD. They have sacrificed us. We wanted peace.

JEREMIAH. Too late!... Why do you put your transgressions on the king's shoulders? You wanted war.

THE CROWD. No!... Not I!... No!... Not I!... It was the king!... Not I!... Not one of us!

JEREMIAH. You all wanted the war, all, all! Your hearts are fickle.... The very ones who are now clamouring for peace, I have myself heard howling for war.... Woe unto you, O people! You drive before every wind. You have fornicated with war, and shall now bear the fruit of war! You have played with the sword, and shall now taste its edge!

The crowd, terrified, clamours for a miracle. Jeremiah refuses. He speaks.

JEREMIAH. Humble yourselves!... Let Jerusalem fall, if God will. Let the temple fall. Let Israel be utterly destroyed and her name wiped out!... Humble yourselves!

The people call him traitor. Jeremiah is seized with a fresh trance. In a transport of love and faith, he welcomes the sufferings inflicted by the beloved hand; he blesses trial, fire, death, shame, the enemy. The people cry aloud: "Stone him! Crucify him!"—Jeremiah stretches out his arms as on the cross. Hungry for martyrdom, he prophesies the Crucified. He wishes to be crucified. And crucified he would be, did not fugitives rush into the square, shouting: "The walls have fallen, the enemy is in the town!"—The mob flees into the temple.

SCENE EIGHT

THE CONVERSION.

In the gloom of a huge crypt we see a prostrate crowd. Here and there groups are formed round an elder reading the Scriptures. Jeremiah stands apart, motionless and as if petrified.—It is on the night following the fall of Jerusalem. Death and destruction are everywhere. The tombs have been violated; the temple has been profaned; all the nobles have been killed, save the king, who has been blinded. Jeremiah groans with horror when he learns that his prophecies have been fulfilled. People draw away from him, as from one accursed. In vain does he, with anguish, defend himself from the charge of having wrought all the evil.

JEREMIAH. I did not will it! You have no right to accuse me. The word came from my mouth as fire from flint. My word is not my will. Force is greater than I. Above me stands He, He, the Terrible One, the Merciless! I am no more than His instrument, His breath, the servant of His malice.... Woe upon the hands of God! Whom He, the

Terrible One seizes, He will never loose.... Let Him set me free! No longer will I speak His words, I will not, I will not....

Trumpets sound without, and the will of Nebuchadnezzar is declared. The city is to disappear from the earth. The survivors may have one night to bury the dead; then they will be carried into captivity. The people lament, refusing to go. But a wounded man, who is in pain, wishes to live, to live! A young woman echoes his words. She does not want to go into the cold, to go to death. Bear anything, suffer anything; but live!—Disputes occur among the crowd. Some say that it is impossible to leave the land where God is. Others maintain that God will be with them wherever they may go. Jeremiah cries despairingly.

JEREMIAH. He is nowhere! Neither in heaven nor in earth, nor in the souls of men!

These sacrilegious words arouse horror. But Jeremiah continues.

JEREMIAH. Who has sinned against Him, if not Himself? He has broken His covenant.... He denies Himself.

Jeremiah recalls all the sacrifices he has made for God. House, mother, friends, he has abandoned all, lost all. He gave himself up wholly to God, serving God because he hoped that God would avert the threatened misfortune. He cursed in the hope that the curse would turn into a blessing. He prophesied in the hope that he was lying, and that Jerusalem would be saved. But his prophecies came true, and God was the liar. He has faithfully served the Faithless One. He refuses to continue this service. He cuts himself off from the God who hates, to join his brothers who suffer. He speaks.

JEREMIAH. I hate Thee, God, and I love them only.

The crowd strikes him, wishing to close his mouth, believing him to be dangerous. He throws himself on his knees, asking pardon for his pride and for his imprecations; he desires to be nothing more than the humblest servitor of his people. But all repulse him as a blasphemer.

At this moment there is a violent knocking at the door. Three envoys from Nebuchadnezzar enter and prostrate themselves before Jeremiah. Nebuchadnezzar, who admires him, wishes to make him chief of the magi. Jeremiah refuses, in disdainful terms. Gradually growing warm as he speaks, he prophecies the fall of Nebuchadnezzar. The great king's hour is at hand, and with fierce joy the prophet heaps curses upon him.

JEREMIAH. The avenger has awakened; He is coming; He draws nigh; terrible are the hands with which He smites.... We are His children, His first-born. He has chastised us, but He will have pity on us. He has thrown us down, but He will set us up again.

The Chaldean envoys flee, affrighted. The people surround Jeremiah and acclaim him. They drink in his frenzied words. God is speaking through his mouth. He unrolls before their eyes the vision of the New Jerusalem, towards which the dispersed tribes will flock from all the quarters of the earth. Peace shines on the city. The peace of the Lord, the peace of Israel. With exclamations of delight, the people, already looking forward to the days of the return, embrace the feet and knees of Jeremiah. The prophet awakens from his trance. He no longer knows what he has said. He is interpenetrated with the love of those around him; he endeavours to restrain their enthusiasm, which is yet further inflamed by a miracle of healing. The true miracle, says Jeremiah, is that he has cursed God and that God has blessed him. God has torn out his hard heart, and has replaced it with a compassionate heart, enabling him to share all suffering and to understand its meaning. "I have been long in finding it; I have been long in finding you, my brothers! No more curses! Sad is our fate; but let us take hope, for life is wonderful, the world is holy. I wish to embrace in my love those whom I have attacked in my anger." He utters thanksgivings for death and for life. Baruch begs him to carry the healing message to the people assembled in the square. Jeremiah agrees to do so, saying: "I have been consoled by God; now let me be the consoler." He wishes to build the undying Jerusalem in the hearts of men.—The people follow him out, calling him God's Master-Builder.

SCENE NINE

THE EVERLASTING ROAD.

The great square of Jerusalem, as in Scene Two, but after the destruction. The half-light of a moon partially veiled by clouds. In the obscurity there can be seen carts, mules, groups of those ready to depart. Voices are heard of persons calling one another and checking their numbers. The people are confused and leaderless. No one pays any attention to the unfortunate Zedekiah, who has been blinded, and whom all curse. Songs are heard, drawing nearer. The singers are in the train of Jeremiah. The prophet speaks to the people, who are at first incredulous and hostile. He consoles them, announcing their divine mission. Their heritage is grief; they are the people of suffering (Leidensvolk), but they are the people of God (Gottesvolk). Happy the vanquished, happy those that have lost all, that they may find God! Glory to the time of trial! From the people, now inspired with enthusiasm, arise choral chants, celebrating the ordeals of ancient days; celebrating Mizraim and Moses.... The choirs break up into groups of voices, now solemn, now gay, now exultant. The whole epic of Israel marches by in these songs, which Jeremiah directs as a skilful driver manages a team. The people, gradually becoming enkindled, wish to suffer, wish to set out for exile, and they call upon Jeremiah to lead them forth. Jeremiah prostrates himself before the unhappy Zedekiah, who has been thrust aside by the crowd. Zedekiah imagines that the prophet is mocking him.

JEREMIAH. Thou hast become the king of sorrows, and never hast thou been more regal.... Anointed by suffering, lead us forth! Thou, who now seest God only, who no longer seest the world, guide thy people!

Turning to the people, Jeremiah shows to them the leader sent by God, the "Crowned-by-Suffering" (Schmerzengekrönte). The people bow before the stricken king.

Day dawns. A tucket sounds. Jeremiah, from the perron of the temple, summons Israel to set out. Let the people fill their eyes with their fatherland, for the last time! "Drink your fill of the walls, drink your fill of the towers, drink your fill of Jerusalem!"—They prostrate themselves, kissing the earth, and lifting a handful to take with them. Addressing the "wandering people" (Wandervolk), Jeremiah tells them to arise, to leave the dead who have found peace, to look not backward but forward, to look out into the distance, to the highways of the world. These highways are theirs. An impassioned dialogue ensues between the prophet and his people.

THE PEOPLE. Shall we ever see Jerusalem again?

JEREMIAH. He who believes, looks always on Jerusalem.

THE PEOPLE. Who shall rebuild the city?

JEREMIAH. The ardour of desire, the night of prison, and the suffering which brings counsel.

THE PEOPLE. Will it endure?

JEREMIAH. Yes. Stones fall, but that which the soul builds in suffering, endureth for ever.

The trumpet sounds once more. The people are now eager to depart. The huge procession ranges itself in silence. At the head is the king, borne in a litter. The tribes follow, singing as they march, with the solemn joy of sacrifice. There is neither haste nor lagging. An infinite on the march. As they pass, the Chaldeans gaze at them with astonishment. Strange folk, whom no one can understand, whether in their dejection or their exultation!

CHORUS OF JEWS. We move among the nations, we move athwart the ages, by the unending roads of suffering. For ever and for ever. Eternally we are vanquished.... But cities fall, nations vanish, oppressors go down into shame. We move onward, through the eternities, towards our country, towards God.

THE CHALDEANS. Their God? Have we not conquered him?... Who can conquer the invisible? Men we can slay, but the God who lives in them we cannot slay. A nation can be controlled by force; its spirit, never.

For the third time the tucket sounds. The sun, breaking forth, shines on the procession of God's people, beginning their march athwart the ages.

*

* *

Thus does a great artist exemplify the supreme liberty of the spirit. Others have made a frontal attack upon the follies and crimes of to-day. At grips with the force which wounds them, their bitter words of revolt bruise themselves against the obstacles they are endeavouring to break down. Here, the soul which has won to peace, sees passing before it the tragical flood of the present. Unperturbed, it torments itself no longer, for its gaze takes in the whole course of the stream, absorbing into itself the secular energies of that stream and the tranquil destiny which leads the flow onward towards the infinite.

November 20, 1917.

Written for the review "Coenobium," edited by Enrico Bignami, at Lugano.

XX

A GREAT EUROPEAN: G. F. NICOLAI[48]

I

ART and science have bent the knee to war. Art has become war's sycophant; science, war's hand-maiden. Few have had the strength or inclination to resist. In art, rare works, sombre French works, have blossomed on the blood-drenched soil. In science, the greatest product during these three criminal years has been the one we owe to G. F. Nicolai, a German whose spirit is free and whose thought has an enormous range.

The book is, as it were, a symbol of that unconquerable Freedom whom all the tyrannies of this age of force have vainly endeavoured to gag. It was written behind prison walls, but these walls were not thick enough to stifle the voice which judges the oppressors and will survive them.

Dr. Nicolai, professor of physiology at Berlin University and physician to the imperial household, found himself, when the war broke out, in the very focus of the madness which seized the flower of his nation. Not merely did he refuse to share that madness. Yet more daring, he openly resisted it. In reply to the manifesto of the 93 intellectuals, published in the beginning of October, 1914, he wrote a counter-manifesto, *An Appeal to Europeans*, which was endorsed by two other distinguished professors at the university of Berlin, Albert Einstein, the celebrated physicist, and Wilhelm Foerster, president of the international bureau of weights and measures, the father of Professor F. W. Foerster. This manifesto was not published, for Nicolai was unable to collect a sufficient number of signatures. In the summer term of 1915 he incorporated it in the opening of a series of lectures he planned to deliver upon the war. Thus, for the fulfilment of what he deemed his duty as an honest thinker, he deliberately risked his social position, his academic career, his distinctions, his comfort, and his friendships. He was arrested, and was interned in Graudenz fortress. There, unaided, and almost without books, he penned his admirable *Biology of War*, and managed to have the manuscript sent to Switzerland, where the first German edition has just been published. The circumstances in which the book was written have an atmosphere of mystery and heroism recalling that of the days when the Holy Inquisition was endeavouring to stifle the thought of Galileo. In the modern world, the Inquisition of the United States of Europe and America is no less crushing than was the Holy Inquisition of old. But Nicolai, firmer of spirit than Galileo, has refused to recant. Last month (September, 1917), the journals of German Switzerland announced that he had been once more brought to trial, and had been sentenced to five months' imprisonment by the Danzig court-martial. Thus again does force manifest its ludicrous weakness, for its unjust decrees merely help to raise a statue to the man whom force would fain strike down.

*

* *

The leading characteristic of book and writer is their universality. The publisher, in a note prefixed to the first edition, tells us that Nicolai "has a world-wide reputation as a physician, more especially in the field of cardiac disease"; that "he is a thinker the universality of whose culture seems almost fabulous in these days of specialisation, for, while distinguished for his knowledge of neokantian philosophy, he is equally at home in literature and in dealing with social problems"; that "he is an explorer who has wandered afoot in China, Malaysia, and even the solitudes of Lapland." Nothing human is foreign to him. In his book, the chapters on universal history, religious history, and philosophical criticism, are closely linked with the chapters on ethnology and biology. What a contrast between this encyclopædic thought, with its reminiscences of our eighteenth century France, and the German savant of caricature, specialist to absurdity—a type which is often enough encountered in real life!

His vast learning is vivified by a captivating and brilliant personality, overflowing with feeling and humour. He makes no attempt to conceal himself behind the mask of a false objectivity. In the Introduction he hastens to tear off this mask, with which the insincere thought of our epoch is covered. He treats with contempt what he calls "the eternal straining for all-round treatment (Einerseits-Andererseits), the perpetual compromise which, under the hypocritical pretext of "justice," weds incompatibles, the carp and the hare, "war and humanity, beauty and fashion, internationalism and nationalism." Method alone should be objective. The conclusions inevitably retain a subjective element, and it is well that this should be so. "As long as we refuse to renounce the right of individuality and the right of striving towards goals of our own choosing, so long must we judge human deeds from the outlook of our own individuality. War is one of the deeds of man, and as such we have to pass judgment on it categorically. Any compromise on this point would obscure the issues; nay, it would be almost immoral.... War, like everything else, should have light thrown upon it from every side before we pass judgment on it; but only to persons of second-rate intelligence can it seem that we should actually pass our judgment on war from all sides at once, or even from two sides only."

Such is the objectivity which we have to expect from this book. Not the soft, flabby, indifferent, contradictory objectivity of the scientific dilettante, of the arch-eunuch: but a mettlesome objectivity which is appropriate in this fighting age, the objectivity of one who honestly attempts to see everything and to know everything; but who, having done so, endeavours to organise his data in accordance with a hypothesis, an intuition tinged with passion.

Such a system is worth precisely what the intuition is worth, precisely what the man who has the intuition is worth. For, in a great thinker, the hypothesis is the man. His hypothesis is the concentrated essence of his energy, his observation, his thought, his imaginative powers, and even of his passions. Nicolai's hypothesis is vigorous, and it takes risks. The central idea of his book may be summed up as follows: "There exists a genus humanum, and there is only one such genus. The human race, humanity as a whole, is but a single organism, and has a common consciousness."

Whoever speaks of a living organism, speaks of transformation and of unceasing movement. This perpetuum mobile gives its peculiar colour to Nicolai's reflections. In general, we who are advocates or opponents of the war tend to pass judgment on it almost exclusively in abstracto. We conceive it as static and absolute. It may almost be said that as soon as a thinker concentrates upon a subject in order to study it, his first step is to kill it. To a great biologist all is movement, and movement is the material of his study. The social or moral question that concerns us is not whether war is good or bad in the sphere of the eternal; but whether war is good or bad for us in our own moment of time. Now, for Nicolai, war is a stage in human evolution which man has long outgrown. His book depicts for us this evolutionary flux of instincts and ideas, an irresistible current in which there is never a backwash.

*

* *

The work is divided into two main parts, of unequal length. The first, occupying three-fourths of the book, is an attack upon the masters of the hour, war, fatherland, and race; an attack upon the reigning sophisms. It is entitled "The Evolution of War." The criticism of the present, in part one, is followed, in part two, by constructive ideas for the future. This second part is entitled "How War may be abolished." It outlines the coming society; sketches its morality and its faith. So abundant, in this book, are data and ideas, that selection is a difficult matter. Apart from the extraordinary richness of its elements, the work may be considered from two outlooks, specifically German, and universally human, respectively. Straightforwardly, at the outset, Nicolai tells his readers that although, in his opinion, all the nations must share responsibility for the war, he proposes to concern himself with the responsibility of Germany alone. He leaves it to the thinkers of other lands, each in his own country, to settle their country's accounts. "It is not my business," he says, "to know whether others have sinned extra muros, but to prevent people from sinning intra muros." If he chooses his instances from Germany above all, this is not because instances are lacking elsewhere, but because he writes, above all, for Germans. A large proportion of his historical and philosophical criticism deals with Germany ancient and modern. The point is well worthy of special analysis. No one, henceforward, will have any right to speak of the German spirit, unless he has read the profound chapters in which Nicolai, endeavouring to define national individuality, analyses the characteristics of German Kultur, analyses its virtues and its vices, its excessive faculty for adaptation, the struggle which the old Teutonic idealism has waged in its conflict with militarism, and elucidates the manner in which idealism was vanquished by militarism. The unfortunate influence of Kant (for whom, none the less, Nicolai has a great admiration) is stressed by him on account of the part it has played in this crisis of a nation's soul. Or rather, we may say, Nicolai stresses the influence of Kant's dualism of the reasons. This dualism of the pure reason and the practical reason (which Kant, despite the best efforts of his later years, was never able to associate in a satisfactory manner) is a brilliant symbol of the contradictory dualism to which modern Germany has accommodated herself all too easily. For Germany, preserving full liberty in the world of thought, has trampled under foot liberty in the world of action, or at least has surrendered this liberty without ever a regret (Chapter Ten, passim).

These analyses of the German soul are of great interest to the psychologist, the historian, and the statesmen. But, since I am compelled to select, I shall choose for description those parts of the book which are addressed to everyone, which touch us all, which are truly universal. I shall speak of the general problem of war and peace in human evolution. I shall have to resign myself to yet further sacrifices. Ignoring the chapters which discuss this topic from a historical and from a literary point of view,[49] I shall confine myself to the biological studies, for it is in these that the author's individuality finds its most original self-expression.

*

* *

At grips with the hydra of war, Nicolai attacks the evil at the root. He opens with a vigorous analysis of instinct in general, for he is careful to avoid denying the innate character of war.

War, he says, is an instinct which springs from the deeps of mankind, an instinct which influences even those who condemn it. It is an intoxication which is carefully fostered in time of peace; when it breaks forth, it takes possession of all alike. But because it is an instinct, it does not follow that this instinct is sacred. Rousseau has popularised the idea that instinct is always good and trustworthy. Nothing of the kind. Instinct may be mistaken. When it is mistaken, the race dies out, and we can therefore easily understand that, in races which do not die out, instinct has a valid reason for existence. Nevertheless, an animal endowed with sound instincts, may be deceived by these instincts when it leaves its primitive environment. We see an example of this in the moth which burns itself in the flame. The instinct was sound in the days when the sun was the only luminary, but no evolution has taken place to adapt this instinct to the existence of lamps. We may admit that every instinct had its use at the time when it first came into existence. This may be true of the fighting instinct, but it does not follow that the combative instinct is useful to man to-day. Instinct is extremely conservative, and survives the circumstances that produced it. For instance, the wolf, wishing to cover up its tracks, buries its excrement; the dog, a town dweller, stupidly scrapes the pavement. In the latter case instinct has become senseless, purposeless.

Man has retained many rudimentary and functionless instincts. He is able to modify them, but in his case the task is peculiarly complex. Man is distinguished from other animals by his incomparably greater power of modifying the natural environment to suit his own purposes. But this being so, man should transform his instincts to adapt them to the changed circumstances. Now these instincts are tenacious, and the struggle is hard. All the more, therefore, is it necessary. Whole species of lower animals became extinct because they were unable to modify their instincts as the environment changed. "Is man also to die out from want of the will to change his instincts? He can change them, or he could if he would. Man alone has the power of choice, and consequently can err. But this curse of the liability to error is the necessary consequence of freedom, and it gives birth to the blessed power man possesses to learn and to transform himself." Yet man makes very little use of this power. He is still encumbered with archaic instincts. He accepts them complacently. He has an excessive esteem for what is old precisely because he is swayed by hereditary instincts which he has unconsciously come to revere.

In the kingdom of the one-eyed, we ought not to make the blind man king. Because we all have combative instincts, it does not follow that we should give these instincts free rein. To-day, when we are realising the advantages of world-wide organisation, it is assuredly time that such instincts should be put under restraint. Nicolai, seeing his contemporaries giving themselves up to their enthusiasm for war, is reminded of dogs which persist in scraping the pavement after relieving nature.

What, precisely, are the combative instincts? Are they essential attributes of the human species? In Nicolai's opinion, they are nothing of the sort. He inclines, rather, to regard them as aberrations, for man was originally a pacific and social animal. His anatomical structure proves it. Man is one of the most defenceless of animals, having neither claws, nor horns, nor hoofs, nor carapace. His ape-like ancestors had no other resource but to seek safety among the branches. When man came down to the ground and took to walking, his hand was freed for other uses. This five-fingered hand, which in most animals has become a weapon (clawed or hoofed), has in the apes alone remained a prehensile organ. Essentially pacific, ill-constructed for striking or tearing, its natural function was to seize and to take.[50] "The hand ... was superfluous as an aid to locomotion on the ground, and thus became free and able to lay hold of something besides trees. Consequently it grasped tools, thus becoming the means and the symbol of man's future greatness." But the hand would not have sufficed for man's defence. Had he been a solitary animal, he would have been destroyed by foes stronger and better equipped than himself. His strength lay in his being gregarious. The social state existed for mankind long before family life began. Men did not voluntarily unite to form a community (the family first, for instance, then the tribe, then a class, then a commune, etc.); it was the existence of the primitive community which rendered possible the advance from the prehuman to the human stage.[51] By nature, as Aristotle said, man is a sociable animal. The drawing together of men is older and more primitive than war.

Look, again, at the lower animals. War is rare between members of the same species. The animals that wage war (stags, ants, bees, and certain birds), have always reached a stage of development in which proprietary rights exist, it may be over booty or it may be over a female. Ownership and war go hand in hand. War is merely one of the innumerable consequences of ownership at a certain stage of evolution. Whatever the declared aim of war, its real purpose always is to despoil man of his labour or of the fruit of his labour. Unless a war be utterly futile, its necessary result will be the enslavement of a part of humanity. Shamefacedly we may change the name, but let us avoid being duped by the new name! A war indemnity is nothing else than part of the labour of the vanquished enemy. Modern war hypocritically pretends to protect private property; but in its effect on the conquered nation as a whole, it indirectly attacks the rights of every individual. Let us be frank. Let us, when we defend war, dare to admit and to proclaim that we are defending slavery.

There is no question of denying that both war and slavery may have been useful, and indeed indispensable, during a certain phase of human evolution. Primitive man, like the lower animals, had all his energies monopolised by the attaining of nutriment. When spiritual needs began to demand their rights, it was necessary that the masses should work to excess in order that a small minority might pass lives of learned leisure. The marvellous civilisations of antiquity could not have existed without slavery. But the time has now arrived when a new organisation has rendered slavery superfluous. In a modern national society a community voluntarily renounces part of its earnings (and will have to renounce an increasingly large part of its earnings) for social purposes. Machines produce about ten times as much as unaided human labour. Were they intelligently used, the social problem would be greatly simplified. A sophism of the political economists assures us that national wellbeing increases proportionally with the increase in the consumption of commodities. The principle is unsound. Its outcome is that it inoculates people with artificial needs. But it is this artificially excited greed which, in the last resort, continues to bolster up slavery in the shape of exploitation and war. Property created war, and property maintains war. For the weak only, is property a source of virtue, since the weak will not make efforts without the stimulus afforded by the desire for possession. Throughout history, war has been for property. Nicolai does not believe that there has ever been a war for a purely ideal object, and without any thought of material domination. People may perhaps fight for the pure ideal of country, in the endeavour to express to the full the genius of their own nation. But the guns will not really help the ideal forward. Such material arguments as guns and bayonets will seem valuable only when the abstract idea has become intertwined with the lusts for power and property. Thus, war, property, and slavery, are close associates. Goethe wrote:

Krieg, Handel und Piraterie
Dreieinig sind sie, nicht zu trennen.[52]

*

* *

Nicolai then proceeds to criticise the pseudo-scientific notions from which our modern intellectuals deduce justifications for war. Above all he disposes of fallacious Darwinism and of the misuse of the idea of the struggle for existence. These notions, imperfectly understood and speciously interpreted, are by many regarded as furnishing a sanction for war. Or, it is held, war is a method of selection, and is therefore a natural right. To such conceptions Nicolai opposes genuine science, the fundamental law of the increase in living beings,[53] and the law that there is a natural limit to growth.[54] It is obvious that the existence of these limitations imposes struggle upon individual beings and upon species, seeing that the world contains only a restricted quantity of energy, that is to say of nutriment. But Nicolai shows that war is the most paltry, the stupidest, one may even say the most ruinous, among all forms of struggle. Modern science, which enables us to estimate the amount of solar energy reaching our planet, shows us that the entire animal world does not as yet make use of more than one twenty thousandth part of the available supply. It is obvious that in these conditions war, that is to say the murder of another accompanied by the theft of that other's share of energy, is an inexcusable crime. It is, says Nicolai, as if loaves were lying about by the thousand, and we were nevertheless to kill a beggar in order to steal his crust. Mankind has an almost boundless field to exploit, and man's proper struggle is the struggle with nature. All other forms of struggle bring impoverishment and ruin, by distracting our attention from our main purposes. The creative method is based upon the harnessing of new and ever new sources of energy. The starting point was the prehistoric discovery of fire, when man for the first time was able to effect the explosive liberation of the solar energy stored up by plants. The discovery marked a new turn in human affairs, and was the dawn of man's supremacy over nature. During the last hundred years this new principle has been developed to such an enormous extent that human evolution has been entirely transformed. Nearly all the chief problems may be said to have been solved, and what remains requisite is the practical application. Thermo-electricity renders possible the direct and purposive utilisation of solar energy. Modern chemical researches point to the possibility of artificially manufacturing foodstuffs, and so on. Were man to apply all his combative energy to the utilisation of the forces of nature, not merely could he live at ease, but there would be room in the world for milliards of additional human beings. When compared with this splendid struggle, how puny seems the great war! What has that war to do with the real struggle for existence? It is a product of degeneration. War is justifiable. Not war between human beings. But creative war for man's mastery over natural forces, the young war of which hardly a millionth part has yet been waged. In this war we can foresee victories such as no human being has ever yet won.

Nicolai, contrasting this creative struggle with the destructive struggle, symbolises them in the persons of two German men of science. One of these is Professor Haber, who has turned his knowledge to account for the manufacture of asphyxiating bombs, and who will doubtless not be forgotten. The other is Emil Fischer, the brilliant chemist who has achieved the synthetic production of sugar, and who will perhaps achieve the synthesis of albumen. Fischer is the founder, or at any rate the forerunner, of the new era of humanity. Future generations will gratefully refer to him as one of the supreme conquerors in the victorious struggle for the sources of life. He is in very truth a practitioner of the "divine art" of which Archimedes spoke.

*

* *

Nicolai's arguments, showing that war is antagonistic to human progress, are confronted with an indisputable fact, a fact which has to be explained—the actual existence of war, and its monstrous expansion. Never has war been more powerful, more brutal, more widespread. Never has war been more glorified. In an interesting chapter (Chapter Fourteen), which introduces a number of debatable points, Nicolai shows that in earlier days apologists for war were exceptional. Even among the epic poets of war, those whose song was of heroism, the direct references to war convey fear and disapproval. Delight in war (Kriegslust), love of war for its own sake, is peculiar to modern literature. We have to come down to the writings of Moltke, Steinmetz, Lasson, Bernhardi, and Roosevelt, to find apotheoses of war, pæans of war whose jubilation is quasi-religious. Nor was it until the outbreak of the present struggle that such huge armies as those of to-day were witnessed. The Greek armies in classical antiquity did not exceed 20,000. Those of imperial Rome, ranged from 100,000 to 200,000. In the eighteenth century, armies of 150,000 were known; while Napoleon had an army of 750,000. In 1870, there were armies of two and a half millions. But in the present war there are ten million fighting men in each camp (Chapter Five and Chapter Six). The increase is colossal, and quite recent. Even if we take into account the possibility of a struggle in the near future between Europeans and Mongols, a proportional increase could not continue beyond a generation or two, for the whole population of the globe would not suffice to furnish such armies.

But Nicolai is not appalled by the titanic dimensions of the monster he is fighting. Indeed, this very fact gives him confidence in the ultimate victory of his cause. For biology has revealed to him the mysterious law of giganthanasia. One of the most important principles of paleontology teaches that all animals (with the exception of insects, which, for this very reason, are, with the brachiopods, the oldest families on the globe), all species, tend throughout the centuries to grow larger and larger until, of a sudden, when they seem greatest and strongest, their forms disappear from the geological record. In nature it is always the large forms that die. That which is large must die for the reason that, in conformity with the imperious law of growth, the day comes when it exceeds the limits of its primordial possibilities. Thus is it, writes Nicolai, with war. Along the boundless field-grey battle lines, thrills the warning of the coming Twilight of the Gods. Everything beautiful and characteristic in the war of ancient days has vanished. Gone is the gay camp life, gone are the motley uniforms, gone is single combat—gone, in a word, are the show features. The battlefield, now, has become little more than an accessory. In former days the scene of battle used to be selected with care, for then the rival armies manœuvred for position. To-day the soldiers settle down haphazard and dig themselves in. The essential work is carried on elsewhere, by the provision of finance, munitions, food supply, railways, etc. In place of the one man of genius as general, we have now the impersonal machinery of the general staff. The old lively, joyous war is dead.—It may be that even yet war has not attained its zenith. In the present war there are still neutrals, and perhaps Freiligrath was right in holding that there must first be some battle in which the whole world will share. But if so, that will be the very last. The final war will be the greatest and the most terrible of all, just as the last of the great saurians was the most gigantic. Our technique has swelled war to its extremest limits, and will then slay war.[55]

*

* *

At bottom, behind its fearsome exterior, the war monster lacks confidence, and feels that its life is threatened. Never before have warmongers appealed, as they appeal to-day, to such a compost of arguments, mystico-scientifico-politico-murderous, to justify the existence of war. No one would dream of such arguments were it not that the days of war are numbered, were it not that the most enthusiastic disciples of war are shaken in their faith. But Nicolai is ruthless in attack, and part of his book is a pitiless satire upon all the sophisms wherewith in our folly we attempt to justify war—the executioner's axe poised over our heads. These sophisms are: the sophism that war is a biological means for ensuring the survival of the fittest; the sophism of defensive war; the sophism of the humanisation of war; the sophism of the alleged solidarity created by war, the so-called party truce; the sophism of the fatherland—for the fatherland, in practical application, becomes the narrowly conceived and artificially constructed political state; the sophism of race; and so on.

I should have been glad to quote numerous extracts from these ironical and severely critical passages. Of exceptional interest are the paragraphs in which he castigates the most impudent and the most flourishing of current sophisms, the sophism of race, for whose sake thousands of poor simpletons of all nations are slaughtering one another. He writes as follows:

"The race problem is one of the most melancholy chapters in the history of human thought. Nowhere else has knowledge, supposedly impartial, consciously or unconsciously placed itself so unscrupulously at the service of ambitious and self-seeking politicians. Indeed, it might almost be said that the various theories of race have never been put forward save with the object of advancing some claim or other. The writings of Houston Stewart Chamberlain, an Anglo-German, afford perhaps the most repulsive example. As we all know, this author has endeavoured to claim as German everyone of outstanding importance in the history of the world, Christ and Dante not excepted. It would be strange if this demagogic example found so [many] imitators.... Recently Paul Souday has attempted to show that all the notable men of Germany belong to the Keltic race ('Le Temps,' August 7, 1915)."

Nicolai replies to these extravagances with the following definite assertions:

1. Proof is lacking that a pure race is better than a mixed race. (Examples are adduced from animal species and from human history.)

2. It is impossible to define the term race as applied to the subdivisions of mankind, for valid criteria are lacking. Such classifications as have been attempted, now upon a historical, now upon a linguistic, and now upon an anthropological basis, are extremely inconsistent one with another, and have been almost complete failures.

3. There are no pure races in Europe. Less than any other nation have the Germans a right to claim racial purity.[56] Anyone who seeks a true Teuton to-day had better go to Sweden, the Netherlands, or England.

4. If to the term race we attach a definite biological meaning, we can hardly say that there is any such thing as a European race.

Patriotism based on race is impossible, and in most cases it is utterly absurd. There is no such thing as ethnic homogeneity in any extant nation. The cohesion of contemporary nations does not come down to them as a heritage of which they can dispose at will. From day to day this cohesion must be rewon. Unremittingly the members of each nation must fortify their community of thought, feeling, and will. This is meet and right. As Renan said, "The existence of a nation should be a daily plebiscite." In a word, what unites people to form a nation is not the force of history; it is the desire to be together, and the mutual need felt by the members of the nation. Our thoughts and our feelings are not guided by the vows that others have made for us, but by our own free will.

Is it so to-day? What place does free will hold among the nations of to-day? Patriotism has assumed an extraordinarily oppressive form.

During no other age in history has it been so tyrannical and so exclusive. It devours everything. Our country, to-day, claims to rank above religion, above art, science, thought, above civilisation. This monstrous hypertrophy cannot be explained as an efflux from the natural sources of patriotic instincts, as an efflux of love of the native soil, of tribal sentiment, of the social need for forming vast communities. Its colossal effects are the outcome of a pathological phenomenon; they are the outcome of mass suggestion. Nicolai tersely analyses this conception. It is remarkable, he says, that whenever several animals or several human beings do anything together, the mere fact of cooperation causes each individual's action to be modified. We have scientific proof that two men can carry far more than twice as much as one. In like manner, a number of human beings react in a very different way from these same beings in isolation. Every cavalryman knows that his horse will do more in the troop than it will do alone, will cover more ground and will suffer less fatigue. Forel has pointed out that an ant which, surrounded by companions, will readily face death, shows fear and runs away from a much weaker ant when she is alone and some way from the ant-hill. Among men, in like manner, the feeling of the crowd greatly intensifies the reactions of each individual. "This is most evident at a public meeting. In many cases the speaker has hardly opened his mouth before he communicates some of his own emotion to every one of his hearers. Suppose it to be only the hundredth part on the average, and suppose that the audience numbers one thousand, then the speaker's emotion has already been multiplied tenfold, as will speedily appear from the reactions of the audience." This in turn reacts on the speaker, who is carried away by the emotions of his hearers. And so it goes on.

Now in our day the audience is of enormous size, and the world war has made it gigantic. Thanks to powerful and rapid means of communication, thanks to the telegraph and the press, the huge groups of allied states have become, as it were, single publics numbered by millions. Imagine, in this vibrant and sonorous mass, the effect of the least cry, of the slightest tremor. They assume the aspect of cosmic convulsions. The entire mass of humanity is shaken as by an earthquake. Under these conditions what happens to such a sentiment as the love of country, originally natural and healthy? In normal times, says Nicolai, a good man loves his country just as he should love his wife, while well aware that there may be other women more beautiful, more intelligent, or better, than she. But one's country to-day is like a hysterically jealous woman who is in a fury when anyone recognises another woman's merits. In normal times the true patriot is (or should be) the man who loves what is good in his country and resists what is evil. But nowadays anyone who acts thus is deemed an enemy of his country. A patriot, in the contemporary sense of the word, loves both what is good and what is bad in his country; he is ready to do evil for the sake of his country; carried away by the stream of mass suggestion, he is positively eager to do evil for his country's sake. The weaker a man's character, the more inflammatory his patriotism. He has no power to resist collective suggestion; and is indeed passionately attracted by it, for every weak man looks for others' support, and believes himself stronger if he does what others are doing. Now, these persons of weak character have no common bond of profound culture. What they need to unite them is an external bond, and what can suit them better than national feeling! "Every blockhead," writes Nicolai, "feels several inches taller if he and a few dozen millions of his kind can only unite to form a majority.... The fewer independent personalities a nation possesses, the fiercer is that nation's patriotism."

This mass attraction, which works like a magnet, is the positive side of jingoism. The negative side is hatred of foreign countries. War is the biological culture-medium. War hurls upon the world sufferings mountain high; it crushes the world by material and spiritual privations. If people are to endure it, there must be a supreme exaltation of mass sentiment, to support the weak by herding them more closely together. This is artificially effected by the newspaper press. The result is appalling. Patriotism concentrates all the energies of the human mind upon love for one's own country and upon hatred for the enemy. Hatred becomes a religion. Hatred without reason, without common sense, and absolutely without foundation. No room is left for any other faculty. Intelligence and morality have abdicated. Nicolai quotes a number of almost incredible examples from the Germany of 1914 and 1915, and equally striking instances could be given in the case of every belligerent nation. There was no resistance to these suggestions. In the collective aberration, all differences of class, education, intellectual or moral value, are reduced to one level; all are equalised. The entire human race, from base to summit, is delivered over to the Furies. If the least sparkle of free will shows itself, it is trampled under foot, and the isolated independent is torn to pieces as Pentheus was torn to pieces by the Bacchantes.

But this frenzy does not disturb the calm vision of the thinker. To Nicolai, the paroxysm he contemplates seems the last flicker of the torch. Just as, he declares, horse-racing and yachting are undergoing their fullest development in our own day, when horses and sails are ceasing to have any practical use, so likewise patriotism has become a fanatical cult at the very moment when it has ceased to be a factor in civilisation. It is the fate of the Epigoni. In remote ages it was good, it was needful, that individual egoism should be broken by the grouping of human beings in tribes and clans. The patriotism of the towns was justified when it victoriously resisted the egoism of the robber barons. The patriotism of the state was justified when it concentrated all the energies of a nation. The national conflicts of the nineteenth century had useful work to do. But to-day the work of the national states is done. New tasks call us. Patriotism is no longer a suitable aim for humanity; its influence is retrograde. But the retrogressive efforts of patriotism are fruitless. No one can arrest the progress of evolution, and people are merely committing suicide by throwing themselves beneath the iron wheels of the chariot. The sage is unperturbed by the frenzied resistance of the forces of the past, for he knows them to be the forces of despair. He leaves the dead to bury their dead; and, looking forward, he already contemplates the living unity of mankind that is to be. Among the trials and disasters of the present, he realises within himself the serene harmony of the "great body" whereof all men are members, as in the profound saying of Seneca: Membra sumus corporis magni.

In a subsequent article we shall learn how Nicolai describes this corpus magnum and the mens magna which animates it, the Weltorganismus, the organism of universal humanity, whose coming is already heralded to-day.

October 1, 1917.

"demain," Geneva, October, 1917.

II

We have seen with how much energy G. F. Nicolai condemns the absurdity of war and the sophisms which serve for its support. Nevertheless the sinister madness triumphs for the time. In 1914, reason went bankrupt. Spreading from nation to nation, this bankruptcy, this madness, subsequently involved all the peoples of the world. There was no lack of established ethical systems and established religions which, had they done their duty, would have opposed a barrier to this contagion of murder and folly. But all the ethical systems, all the religions, now in existence, proved hopelessly inadequate. We have seen it for ourselves in the case of Christianity; and Nicolai shows, following Tolstoi, that Buddhism is in no better case.

As far as Christianity is concerned, its abdication is of old date. After the great compromise under Constantine, in the fourth century of our era, when the emperor made the church of Christ a state church, the essential thought of Jesus was betrayed by the official representatives of the creed, and was delivered over to Cæsar. Only among certain free religious individualities, most of whom were charged with heresy, was this essential thought preserved (to a degree) until our own time. But its last defenders have lately denied it. The Christian sects which up to now have invariably refused military service, for example the Mennonites in Germany, the Dukhobors in Russia, the Paulicians, the Nazarenes, etc., are participating in the war to-day.[57] "Simon Menno, the founder of the Mennonites, who died in 1561, condemned war and vengeance.... As late as 1813, the strength of moral conviction in the members of this sect was still so great that, despite the patriotic excitement of that year, so ruthless a soldier as York actually exempted them from Landwehr service, by a decree dated February 18th. But in 1915, H. G. Mannhardt, Mennonite preacher in Danzig, delivered an address glorifying feats of arms and martial heroes."

"There was a time," writes Nicolai, "when it was believed that Islam was inferior to Christianity. At that date the Turkish armies were threatening the heart of Europe. To-day the Turk has almost been driven out of Europe, but morally he has conquered Europe. Unseen, the green flag of the Prophet floats over every house in which there is talk of the 'holy war.'"

German religious poems depict the fight in the trenches as "a test of piety instituted by God." No one is now astonished at the absurd contradiction in terms involved in speaking of "Christian warfare." Few theologians or churchmen have dared to swim against the stream. In his admirable book *La Guerre infernale*,[58] Gustave Dupin has pilloried gruesome specimens of militarist Christianity. Nicolai gives other samples, which it would be a pity to leave unrecorded. In 1915, Professor Baumgarten, a Kiel theologian, placidly pointed out that there is opposition between the morality of bellicose nationalism and the morality of the Sermon on the Mount, but "at present," he went on to say, "we ought to pay more attention to Old Testament texts"; thus deliberately, and with a smile, throwing Christianity overboard. Arthur Brausewetter, another theologian, made a remarkable discovery. War revealed to him the Holy Spirit. "Never, till this year of war, 1914, did we really know the nature of the Holy Ghost...."

While Christianity was thus publicly denied by its priests and its pastors, the religions of Asia were no less ready to jettison the inconvenient thoughts of their founders. Tolstoi had already pointed this out. "The Buddhists of to-day do not merely tolerate murder; they positively justify it. During the war between Japan and Russia, Soyen Shaku, one of the leading Buddhist dignitaries in Japan, wrote a defence of war.[59] Buddha had uttered this beautiful word of afflicted love: 'All things are my children, all are images of myself, all flow from a single source, and all are parts of my own body. That is why I cannot rest as long as the least particle of what is has failed to reach its destination.' In this sigh of mystical love, which aspires towards the fusion of all beings, the Buddhist of to-day has safely discovered an appeal to a war of extermination. For, he declares, inasmuch as the world has failed to reach its destination, has failed owing to the perversity of many men, we must make war on these men and must annihilate them. 'Thus shall we extirpate the roots of evil.'"—This bloodthirsty Buddhist recalls to my mind the guillotine-idealism of our Jacobins in '93. Their monstrous faith is summed up in the words of Saint-Just which close my tragedy *Danton*:

"The nations slay one another that God may live."[60]

When religions are so weak, it is not surprising that mere ethical systems should prove unavailing. Nicolai shows us what a travesty Kant's disciples have made of their master's teaching. Willy-nilly, the author of the *Critique of Pure Reason* has been compelled to put on the field-grey uniform. Have not his German commentators insisted that the Prussian army is the most perfect realisation of Kant's thought? For, they tell us, in the Prussian army the sentiment of Kantian duty has become a living reality.

Let us waste no more time over these inanities, which differ only in shade from those made use of in every land by the national guard of the intelligentsia, to exalt their cause and to glorify war. Enough to recognise, with Nicolai, that European idealism crashed to ruin in 1914. The German writer's conclusion (which I am content to record without comment), is that "we have proof that ordinary idealistic morality, whether Kantian or Christian, is absolutely useless, for it is unable to lead any of those who profess it to act morally." In view of the manifest impossibility of founding moral action upon a purely idealistic basis, Nicolai considers that our first duty is to seek some other basis. He wishes that Germany, schooled by her ignominious fall, by her "moral Jena," should work at this task whose fulfilment is so indispensable to mankind—should work at it for herself even more than for any other nation, seeing that her need is the greatest. "Let us see," he says, "if it be not possible to find in nature, scientifically studied, the conditions of an objective ethic, of an ethic that shall be independent of our personal sentiments, good or bad, always vacillating."

*

* *

In the first part of the volume we have learned that war is a transitional phenomenon in human evolution. What, then, is the true and eternal principle of humanity? Is there such a principle? Is there a higher imperative, valid for all men alike?

Yes, answers Nicolai. This higher imperative is the very law of life, which governs the entire organism of humanity. Natural law has only two bases, only two which can never be shaken: the individual, separately considered; and the human universality. All intermediaries, like the family and the state, are organised groupings,[61] subject to change, and they do actually change with changing customs; they are not natural organisms. Egoism and altruism, the two powerful sentiments which give life to our moral world, acting therein like the contrasted forces of positive and negative electricity, are the respective expressions of the individual and of the collectivity. Egoism is the natural outflow of our individuality. Altruism owes its existence to the obscure recognition that we are parts of a united organism, humanity.

In the second half of his book Nicolai undertakes to throw light upon this obscure realisation, and to establish it upon a scientific foundation. He undertakes to show that humanity is no mere abstraction, but a living reality, an organism that can be subjected to scientific observation.

In this study, the poetical intuition of the ancient philosophers is interestingly linked with the experimental spirit and the analytical method of modern science. The latest biological and embryological theories are invoked to help in the comment on the hylozoism of the seven sages and the mysticism of the early Christians. Janicki and de Vries shake hands with Heraclitus and Saint Paul. The upshot is a strange vision of materialistic and dynamistic pantheism—a vision of humanity considered as a body and a soul in unceasing motion.

Nicolai begins by reminding us that this idea has existed in all ages. He summarises the history of the doctrine. We have the "fire" of Heraclitus, which for the sage of Ephesus was also the universal intelligence of the world. We have the same thing in the "pneuma" of the stoics and in the "pneuma agion" of the primitive Christians, the sacred energy, the vivifying force, which is the concentrated essence of all the souls. It is what Origen speaks of as "universum mundum velut animal quoddam immensum." We encounter the idea once more in the fertile fancies of Cardanus, Giordano Bruno, Paracelsus, and Campanella. Animistic ideas are mingled with the science of

Newton, and permeate his hypothesis of universal gravitation. Indeed, Musschenbroek, his immediate disciple, describes the gravitative principle as "amicitia"; while Lichtenberg tells us that it is the "longing of the heavenly bodies for one another!" In a word, through the whole development of human thought runs the belief that our world is a single organism with a consciousness of its own. Nicolai tells us how it would interest him to write the history of this idea; and he outlines that history in his fascinating fourteenth chapter, "The Evolution of the Idea of the World as Organism."[62]

He then passes to scientific demonstration. Is there, he asks, a material bond, a bodily, living, and enduring tie, between human beings of all lands and all ages?[63] He finds a proof that there is such a bond in the researches of Weismann and in that writer's theory of the germ plasm, which has now become classic.[64] In each individual, the cells of the germ plasm continue the life of the parents, of which, in the fullest sense of the word, they are living portions. They are undying. They pass, changeless, to our children and to our children's children. Thus there really persists throughout the whole genealogical tree a part of the same living substance. A portion of this organic unity lives in each individual and thereby we are physically connected with the universal community. Nicolai points out, in passing, the remarkable relationships between these scientific hypotheses of the last thirty years and certain mystical intuitions of the Greeks and the early Christians—"the spirit (pneuma) that quickeneth" (Saint John, vi, 63), the generative spirit, which is not only distinguished from the flesh, as Saint John declares, but is likewise distinguished from the soul, as appears from a passage in Saint Paul's first epistle to the Corinthians (xv, 44), where the "spiritual body" (soma pneumatikon) is contrasted with the "natural body" (soma psuchikon). The spiritual body is declared to be more essential than the natural body (the psychical or intellectual body); and the former really and materially penetrates the bodies of all men.

Nor is this all. The studies made by contemporary biologists, and notably by the Russian biologist Janicki, on sexual reproduction[65] have explained how this method of reproduction safeguards the homogeneity of the germ plasm in an animal species, and how it unceasingly renews the mutual contacts among the individual members of a race. Janicki writes: "The world, if I may say so, has not been broken up into a mass of independent fragments, which then, for ever isolated one from another, ... must strike out for themselves on straight courses, with only side branches. On the contrary, owing to bi-sexual reproduction (amphimixis), the image of the macrocosm is ... reflected as a microcosm in each part; and the macrocosm resolves itself into a thousand microcosms.... Thus the individuals, while remaining independent, are materially and continuously interconnected, like strawberry plants whose runners are joined together.... Each separate individual develops, as it were, through an invisible system of rhizomes (subterranean roots) which unite the germ substances of countless individualities."—Thus it has been calculated that in the twenty-first generation, in five hundred years let us say, and supposing an average of three children to each couple, the posterity of a single couple will be equal in number to the entire human race. It may, therefore, be said that each one of us has within him a small portion of the living substance belonging to every one of the human beings that were living five hundred years ago. Consequently it is absurd that anyone should wish to restrict an individual, be he whom he may, within the category of a separate nation or race.

Let us add that thought, too, propagates itself throughout mankind, in like manner with the germ plasm.

Every thought, once expressed, leads in the human community a life independent of its creator; undergoes development in other minds; and has, like the germ plasm, an immortal life. So that, in humanity, there is neither true birth nor true death, whether material or spiritual. Empedocles, of old, realised this, for he said:

"Yet another truth will I tell unto thee. Not a mortal thing is truly born, and death the destroyer is not the end. There is nought but intermixture and exchange of what is intermixed. But among men it is customary to term this 'birth.'"

Humanity, therefore, materially and spiritually, is a single organism; all its parts are intimately connected and share in a common development.

Upon these ideas there must now be grafted the concept of mutation and the observations of Hugo de Vries.—If this living substance which is common to all humanity should, at any time and owing to any influence, have acquired the capacity for changing[66] after a certain lapse of time, for instance a thousand years, then all those beings which have in them a share of this substance may suddenly undergo identical changes. It is well known that Hugo de Vries has observed such sudden variations in plants.[67] After centuries of stability in the characteristics of a species, quite suddenly, in a great number of individuals belonging to this species, there will one year occur a modification, the leaves becoming longer, or shorter, etc. Thenceforward this modification will be propagated as a constant feature, so that, by the following year, a new species will have come into existence.—The same thing happens among human beings, especially in the human brain; for, as far as man is concerned, the most striking instances of variation are found in the psychic domain. In each year, certain human beings present brain variations. Such abnormal individuals are sometimes regarded as madmen and sometimes as men of genius. They herald the coming variations of the species, variations of which they are the forerunners. At due date, the same peculiarities will suddenly manifest themselves throughout the species. Experience shows that transformations, or moral and social discoveries, appear at the same moment in the most widely separated and the most various countries. I have myself often been struck by this fact, both when studying history and when observing the men of my own day. Contemporary societies, at a great distance one from another and having no means of rapid intercommunication, will simultaneously exhibit the same moral and social phenomena. Hardly ever is a discovery born in the brain of a single inventor. At the same instant, other inventors happen upon it, anticipate it, or are hot upon the trail. The popular phrase runs, "the idea is in the air." When an idea is in the air, a mutation is about to occur in the human brain. We are, says Nicolai, on the eve of a "mutation of war." Moltke and Tolstoi represent the two great contrasted variations in human thought. Moltke extolled the ethical value of war; Tolstoi passed unqualified condemnation on war. Which of these two minds represents the variation of genius and which the variation of madness? In the light of contemporary events, most people would be inclined to give the palm to Moltke. But when an organism is about to undergo mutation, the change is often preluded by frequent and extensive variations. Of these divergent variations, those only persist which are best suited to the conditions of existence. Thus, in Nicolai's view, the ideas of Moltke and his disciples are a favourable presage that mutation is imminent.

*

* *

Whatever we may think of this hope that within the near future a mutation will occur leading to the formation of a humanity radically opposed to war, it is enough to watch the biological development of the extant world to acquire the belief that a new organisation, vaster and more peaceful, is at hand. In proportion as humanity evolves, communications between men are multiplied. During the last century there occurred a sudden and enormous improvement in the technical means for the exchange of ideas. To give one example only. In former days the circulation of letters throughout the whole world did not exceed one hundred thousand a year. To-day, the postal correspondence in Germany amounts to a milliard letters a year (15 per head), whereas formerly the number was 1 per 1,000 of the population. About forty years ago, in the countries which now form parts of the postal union, three milliards of letters, etc., were posted annually. By the year 1906 the number had increased to thirty-five milliards; and by 1914, to fifty milliards. (In Germany, 1 per head every 10 days; in Great Britain, 1 per head every 3 days.) We have further to consider the increased speed of communication. Distance no longer exists for the telegraph; "the entire civilised world has become a large room in which we can all talk with one another."

Such changes cannot fail to influence social life. In earlier times, any thought of union or federation between the various states of Europe remained utopian, were it only on account of the difficulty and slowness of communications. As Nicolai says, a state cannot extend to infinite proportions; it must be able to act promptly upon the different parts of its organism. To a certain extent, therefore, its size is a function of the rapidity of communications. In prehistoric times, a traveller could cover only about 12 miles a day; when wheeled traffic became established, the daily postal journey extended to 60 miles, and in the later days of mail-coach development, this distance was more than doubled; towards 1850, the railway service was able to cover 375 miles a day; modern trains range to 1,250 miles a day; an express service covering 6,000 miles or more a day is already within the scope of technical possibilities. For barbarians, the country was limited to a mountain valley. The states that existed at the close of the middle ages, states which have not greatly varied down to our times, were adapted in size to the possibilities of the mail coach. Now, such petty states are far too small. The modern man will no longer consent to be restricted in this way. He is continually crossing frontiers. He wants vast states, like those of America, Australia, Russia, or South Africa. We look forward to the days when, be it only for material reasons like the foregoing, the whole world will be a single state. Nothing that we can do will check this evolution; the change will come whether we like it or not. We can now understand that all earlier attempts to unite the nations of Europe, all those initiated in the middle ages and continued down to the nineteenth century, were rendered impossible of achievement by the lack of suitable material conditions. With the best will in the world, their realisation was impossible. But the requisite conditions exist to-day, and we may say that the organisation of contemporary Europe no longer corresponds to its biological development. Willy-nilly, Europe will have to adapt itself to the new conditions. The days of European unity have come. And the days of world-wide unity are at hand.[68]

The new body of humanity, the "corpus magnum" of which Seneca spoke, needs a soul, and it needs a new faith. This faith, while retaining the absolute character of the old religions, must be wider and more plastic than they; it must not merely be adapted to the existing needs of the human mind, but must take into account the possibilities of future development. All previous religions, rooted in tradition and wishing to bind man to the past, were encased in dogmatism; and they one and all, as time passed, became hindrances to natural evolution. Where can we find a basis for faith and morals which shall be simultaneously absolute and mutable; shall be above man, and none the less human; shall be ideal, and none the less real?—We shall find what we want, says Nicolai, in humanity itself. For us, humanity is a reality which develops throughout the ages, but which at every moment represents for us an absolute entity. It evolves in a direction which may be fortuitous, but which, once taken, cannot be changed. It simultaneously embraces the past, the present, and the future. It is a unity in time, a vast synthesis of which we are but fragments. To be human, means to understand this development, to love it, to trust one's hopes to it, and to endeavour to participate in it consciously. Herein we find an ethical system, which Nicolai sums up as follows:

1. The community of mankind is the divine upon earth, and is the foundation of morals.

2. To be a man is to feel within one's self the reality of humanity at large. It is to feel, like a living law, that we are elements of that greater organism, in which (to quote Saint Paul's admirable intuition) we are all parts of one body and every one members one of another.

3. The love of our neighbour is a feeling of good health. A general love for humanity is the feeling of organic health in humanity at large, reflected in one of its members. Therefore we should love and honour the human community and everything which sustains and fortifies it—work, truth, good and sound instincts.

4. Fight everything which injures it. Above all, fight bad traditions, instincts that have become useless or harmful.

*

* *

"Scio et volo me esse hominem," writes Nicolai at the close of his book. "I know that I am a man, and I wish to be one."

Man—he understands by this a being aware of the ties which attach him to the great human family, and aware of the evolution which carries him along with it—a spirit which understands and loves these ties and these laws, and which, submitting to them with delight, thereby becomes free and creative.[69] Man—the term applies to Nicolai himself in the sense of the character in Terence's play who said, "Homo sum; humani nihil a me alienum puto." Herein lies the great merit of his work; and herein, too, we find its defect. In his eagerness to include everything, he has attempted the impossible. He speaks in one place with an unjust contempt, and with a contempt which he above all should have been slow to express, of the "Vielwisser," the polyhistor.[70] But he himself is a Vielwisser, one of the finest specimens of this genus, too rare in our day. In all domains, art, science, history, religion, and politics, his insight is penetrating, but at the same time rapid and incisive. Everywhere his opinions are lively, often original, and often debatable. The wealth of his glimpses "de omni re scibili," the abundance of his intuitions and his reasonings, have a brilliant and at times a venturesome character. The historical chapters are not above reproach. Unquestionably the lack of books accounts for certain insufficiencies, but I think the peculiarities of the author's own genius are partly responsible. He is headlong and impulsive. These qualities give charm to his writing, but they are dangerous. What he loves, he sees beautifully. But woe to what he does not love! Take, for instance, his disdainful and hasty judgments upon the recent imaginative writers of Germany—judgments passed wholesale.[71]

It is a remarkable fact that this German biologist resembles no one living or dead so much as he resembles one of our French encyclopedists of the eighteenth century. I know no one in contemporary France who can, to the same degree, be compared with him. Diderot and Dalembert would have opened their arms to this man of science, who humanises science, who boldly limns a picture instinct with life, a brilliant synthesis of the human mind, of its evolution, of its manifold activities, and of the results it has achieved; who throws wide the doors of his laboratory to intelligent men of the world; and who deliberately wishes to make of science an instrument of struggle and emancipation in the war of the nations on behalf of liberty. Like Dalembert and Diderot, he is "in the thick of the fight." He marches in the vanguard of modern thought, but he does not go further ahead than the due distance between a leader and his followers; he is never isolated, as were those great forerunners who remained throughout life cloistered in prophetic visions, centuries away from realisation; his ideals are no more than a day in advance of those cherished by his contemporaries.

A German republican, he looks no higher for the moment than the political ideals of Young America, the America of 1917, in which (according to Nicolai) "we can see, not merely what this new, so to speak, cosmopolitan, patriotism means, but also the limits which must still be imposed on it.... The day for the brotherhood of man has not yet come [we quote Nicolai, remember]; the time is not yet ripe. There is still too profound a cleavage between White, Yellow, and Black. It is in America that European patriotism has awakened, the sentiment which will undoubtedly be the patriotism of the near future, and whose heralds we would fain be.... The new Europe is already born, though not in Europe."[72]

In these lines we discern Nicolai's limitations, which any eighteenth century cosmopolitan would have over-stepped. In the practical domain, our author is essentially, uniquely, but absolutely, a European. It was to Europeans that he addressed his Manifesto of October, 1914, and his book of 1915.

"It seems to us necessary before everything else," he writes, "that there should be a union of all who are in any way attached to European civilisation, that is to say, who are what Goethe once almost prophetically called 'good Europeans.'" And in a note he adds: "By European civilisation I mean every endeavour, in the broadest sense of the word, throughout the world, the origin of which can ultimately be traced back to Europe."

Much might be said concerning this curtailment. For my own part, I consider it neither right nor useful that humanity should draw a line of demarcation between civilisation of European origin and the lofty civilisations of Asia. In my view, the harmonious realisation of humanity can be secured in no other way than by the union of these great complementary forces. Nay more; I believe that the European soul, unaided, impoverished and scorched by centuries of spendthrift existence, would be likely to flicker and even to go out, unless regenerated by an influx of the thought of other races.—But to each day its own task. Nicolai, at once thinker and man of action, turns to the most immediate duty. Concentrating all his energies upon a single aim, he accelerates the moment of attainment. "Just as certain of our forefathers, in advance of their time, enthusiastically advocated a united Germany, even so do we mean to fight for a united Europe. That is the hope inspiring this book."[73]—Nor does he merely hope for the victory of this cause. He already enjoys the victory, by anticipation. Immured in Graudenz fortress, near the room where Fritz Reuter, the German patriot, spent years in captivity because he believed in Germany, Nicolai notes that the Reuter room has been converted into a sanctuary by his erstwhile gaolers, "which is a living instance of the fact that reaction cannot endure for ever." His mind reverting to his own case, he declares: "We may be quite sure that the very same persons who to-day still continue to decry as high treason Goethe's conception of the citizen of Europe, will in a few years' time themselves subscribe to it."

This confidence radiates from every page of the book. It is Nicolai's faith in the future which influences us even more than the writer's ideas. That faith is a stimulant and a moral tonic. It awakens us and sets us free. Those of kindred spirit group themselves round him because, in the dark places of the earth where they wander chilled and with faltering steps, he is a focus of joy and fervid optimism. This prisoner, this man under sentence, smiles as he contemplates the force which thinks it has conquered him, the force of reaction let loose, and of unreason, overthrowing that which he knows to be right and true. Precisely because his faith is violated, he desires to proclaim it. "Precisely because war is in progress, I wish to write a book of peace." Thinking of his brothers in the faith, weaker and more broken, he dedicates to them this book "to assure them that the war is but a passing phase; that we must be careful not to attach too much importance to it." He speaks, he tells us, "to inspire fair-minded and right-thinking men with my own triumphant assurance."[74]

May he be a model to us! May the small and persecuted band of those who refuse to share the general hatred, and whom therefore hate persecutes, be ever warmed by this inward joy! Nothing can deprive them of it. Nothing can harm them. For, amid the horror and the shames of the present, they are the contemporaries of the future.

October 15, 1917.

"demain," Geneva, November, 1917.

XXI

REFLECTIONS ON READING AUGUSTE FOREL

THE name of Auguste Forel is renowned in the world of European science, but within the confines of his own land his writings are perhaps less well known than they should be. Every one is familiar with the social activities of this splendid personality, of this man whose indefatigable energies and ardent convictions have not been affected either by his age or by ill-health. But Latin Switzerland, which justly admires the writings of the naturalist J. H. Fabre, hardly seems to realise that in Forel it is fortunate enough to possess an observer of nature whose insight is no less keen than that of Fabre, and whose scientific endowments are perchance even richer and more unerring. I have recently been reading some of Auguste Forel's studies of ant life, and I have been profoundly impressed by the wide scope of his experimental researches, carried on for a whole lifetime.[75] While patiently observing and faithfully describing the life of these insects, day by day, hour by hour, and year after year, his thoughts have been simultaneously directed towards the ultimate recesses of nature, so that he has been able from time to time to raise for a moment a corner of that veil of mystery which covers our own instincts.

Here is a strange fact. J. H. Fabre believes in providence, "le bon Dieu"; Auguste Forel is a monist, a psycho-physicist. Nevertheless, Forel's observations suggest to the reader a conception of nature which is far less crushing than that suggested by the observations of Fabre. The latter, untroubled by anxieties concerning the human soul, sees in the little insects he is studying nothing more than marvellous machines. But Forel discerns here and there sparks of reflective consciousness, germs of individual will. These are no more than widely separated luminous points, piercing the darkness. But the phenomenon is all the more impressive for its rarity. I have amused myself by selecting from out this wealth of observations a group of facts wherein are displayed the secular instincts, the "anagke," of the species—oppugned, shattered, vanquished. Wherefore should a combat of this sort be less dramatic when waged by these humble ants than when it is waged by the Atrides in

Orestes? In all cases alike, we have the same waves of force, blind or conscious; the same interplay of light and shade. And the analogy of certain social phenomena, as we observe them among these myriads of tiny beings, and as we observe them among ourselves, may help us to understand ourselves—and perhaps to achieve self-command.

I shall be content, here, to cull from the vast experimental repertory of Auguste Forel, those of his observations which bear upon certain psychopathological collective states, and those which bear upon the formidable problem which faces us to-day, the problem of war.

*

* *

Ants, says Forel, are to other insects what man is to other mammals. Their brain surpasses that of all other insects in its relative size and in the complexity of its structure. Even if they fail to attain the level of individual intelligence characteristic of the higher mammals, nevertheless they excel all animals without exception in the development of their social instincts. It is not surprising therefore, that in many respects their social life should resemble that of the human species. Like the most advanced human communities, the ant societies are democracies, fighting democracies. Let us contemplate them at work.

The Ant State is not restricted to the single ant-hill; it has its territory, its domain, its colonies. Like our colonising powers, it has its ports of call, its revictualling stations. The territory is a single meadow, a few trees, or a hedge. The domain of exploitation consists of the ground and the subsoil, together with the aphis-bearing trees whence the ants take the aphides they keep under domestication. Their colonies are detached nests more or less distant from the metropolis and more or less numerous (there may be as many as two hundred), communicating with the primary nest by open roads or by underground passages. The depots are small nests or dug-outs for the use of ants on long expeditions, ants that require a rest or those that are overtaken by bad weather.

Naturally these communities tend to grow, and they thus come into conflict one with another. "Territorial disputes, along the frontier between two great ant communities, are the usual cause of embittered struggles. The aphis-bearing shrubs are the most fiercely contested. But, in the case of certain species, subterranean domains (the roots of plants) are likewise the region of savage warfare." Some species live solely by war and plunder. Polyergus rufescens (Huber's "amazon") disdains work, and has indeed lost the power. The members of this species live as slave-owners, served, tended, fed, by troops of slaves, the latter being recruited (in the larval or pupal stage) by slave raids upon neighbouring ant-hills.

Thus war is endemic, and every citizen of these democracies, every worker ant, has to take part in the fighting. In certain species (Pheidole pallidula), the military caste is distinct from the working caste. The soldier takes no part in domestic work, but idles away the days in barracks, with nothing to do save at the times when life has to be staked for the defence of the community.[76] There are no leaders, or at any rate no permanent leaders. We see neither kings nor generals. The expeditionary armies of Polyergus rufescens, which may vary from one hundred thousand to two hundred thousand ants, act in obedience to streams of influence which appear to emanate from small and scattered groups, sometimes in the van and sometimes in the rear. When the army is on the march, the entire column will suddenly halt, remaining indecisive and motionless, as if paralysed. Of a sudden, the initiative will be taken by some small group of ants whose members rush about among the others, striking these on the head; then the temporary leaders start off, and the whole army is in motion once more.

Formica sanguinea is an able tactician. Forel follows Huber in his description of the fighting methods of this species. The insects do not advance in close formation, à la Hindenburg, but in platoons, communicating one with another by orderlies. They do not make a frontal attack; but, after watching the enemy's movements, attempt to take him by surprise on the flank. Their aim, like that of Napoleon, is to concentrate upon a given point at a particular time, to secure there and then the advantage of numbers. Like Napoleon, too, they know how to lower the adversary's morale. Seizing the psychological moment when the enemy's courage or confidence flags, they hurl themselves upon him with irresistible fury, now recking nought of numbers, for they know that at such a time one fighter on their own side is worth a hundred on the other, where panic is rife. Moreover, like good soldiers, their aim is not to kill, so much as to gain the victory and to harvest its fruits. When the battle is won they post a guard at each exit of the conquered nest. The members of this guard allow the enemy ants to escape, provided these carry nothing away. The victors pillage to the uttermost, but do as little killing as possible.

Between species of equal strength, fighting for frontiers, war is not perennial. After many days of battle and glorious hecatombs, the rival states would appear to recognise that their respective ambitions are unattainable. As if by common consent, the armies withdraw within either side of a frontier, which is accepted by both parties with or without treaty. This frontier is respected much more perfectly than among men, bound merely by "scraps of paper." The citizen ants of the two communities always keep strictly within their borders.

*

* *

A matter of even greater interest is to note how this war-making instinct originates among our brothers the insects; to study how it develops; and to ascertain whether it is fixed or modifiable. Here Forel's observations and experiments lead to the most remarkable deductions.

J. H. Fabre, in a famous passage of *Insect Life*,[77] tells us that "brigandage is the law in the struggle among living beings.... In nature, murder is universal. Everywhere we encounter a hook, a dagger, a spear, a tooth, nippers, pincers, a saw, horrible clamps, ..." But he exaggerates. He has a keen eye for the facts of mutual slaughter and mutual devouring, but he fails to see the facts of mutual aid and associated effort. Kropotkin has devoted an admirable book to the study of phenomena of the latter class, as manifested throughout nature.[78] Furthermore, the careful observations of Forel show that in ants the instincts of war and plunder may be modified or overcome by instincts of a contrary character.

First of all, Forel proves that the war-making instinct is not fundamental. This instinct does not exist in the early stages of ant life. Putting together newly hatched ants belonging to three different species, Forel obtained a mixed ant community whose members lived in perfect harmony. The only primitive instinct of newly hatched ants is that for domestic work and the care of larvae. "Not until later do ants learn to distinguish between friend and foe; not until later do they realise that they are members of a single ant community on behalf of which they have to fight."[79]

Forel next presents the fact, even more surprising, that the intensity of the warrior instinct is directly proportional to the size of the collectivity. Two ants of enemy species meeting at a distance from their respective nests or from their own folk, will avoid one another and run away in opposite directions. Even if you come across the armies in full combat, and you remove from the ranks an ant belonging to either side and shut the two by themselves in a small box, they will do one another no harm. If, instead of taking merely two, you shut up a moderate number from either side within a narrow space, they will fight half-heartedly for a while, but soon cease to struggle, and often end by making friends. In such circumstances, says Forel, they will never resume the struggle. But put these same ants back among the fighting forces of their respective sides, and separate them by a reasonable distance, so that they might live at peace, and you will see them return to the attack; the individuals which a moment before were avoiding one another with repugnance or fear, will now furiously engage in mutual slaughter.[80] It thus appears that the combative instinct is a collective contagion.

Sometimes this epidemic assumes unmistakably morbid attributes.[81] In proportion as it extends and in proportion as the struggle is prolonged, the fighting rage becomes a positive frenzy. The very same ant, which at the outset was timid, will now be affected with a paroxysm of furious madness. She no longer knows what she is about. She throws herself upon her own companions, kills the slaves that are endeavouring to calm her, bites everything she touches, bites fragments of wood, can no longer find her way. Other members of the community, slaves as a rule, have to surround such a frenzied worker by twos and threes; they seize her by the legs and caress her with their antennae until she comes to herself, has recovered as I might say "her reason." Why not? Had she not lost it?

We have hitherto been dealing exclusively with general phenomena, those which obey fairly rigid laws. Now we are faced with special phenomena wherein initiative conflicts in the most peculiar way with the instinct of the species, and, which is yet more curious, in the end causes instinct to stray from its appointed path, and even to die out altogether.

Forel places in a jar some ants of enemy species, the sanguinea and the pratensis. After a few days of warfare, followed by a sullen armistice, he introduces a newly hatched pratensis which is very hungry. She runs to those of her own species begging them to feed her. The pratenses fob her off. Then the poor innocent appeals to the enemies of her species, the sanguineae, and, after the manner of ants, she licks the mouth of two among them. The two sanguineae are so touched by this gesture, which turns their instinct topsy-turvy, that they disgorge their honeyed store and feed the young enemy. Thenceforward all is well. An offensive and defensive alliance is formed between the little pratensis and the sanguineae against the ants of the young one's own species. The alliance becomes irrevocable.

Let me adduce another example; the results of a common danger. Forel places in a bag a nest of sanguineae and another of pratenses. He shakes them together, and leaves them in the bag for an hour. Thereafter he opens the bag and places it in direct contact with an artificial nest. At first we witness a general state of confusion, a delirium of fear. The ants cannot recognise one another apart; they show their mandibles, and then sidle away in a panic. But by degrees calm is restored. The sanguineae begin by removing the pupae, taking indifferently those of both species. Some of the pratenses follow their example. From time to time fights take place, but these are merely single combats, and they grow less and less fierce. From the next day onwards, all work together. In four days the pact is sealed; the pratenses disgorge food to the sanguineae. At the end of a week, Forel transports them to the neighbourhood of an abandoned ant-hill. They settle in, helping one another in the house-moving, carrying one another, and so forth. No more than a few isolated individuals of the respective species, irreconcilable nationalists no doubt, keep up their sacred enmity, and end by killing one another. A fortnight later, the mixed community is flourishing; perfect concord prevails. The summit of the ant-hill, which at ordinary times is covered with pratenses for the most part, reddens with the martial sanguineae directly danger threatens the common state. Next month, Forel, carrying the experiment a stage further, went to the old nest for a number of the pratenses and put them down just outside the hill of the mixed community. The newcomers promptly fell upon the sanguineae. But these latter defended themselves without animosity, merely knocking the aggressors head over heels, and then letting them alone. The pratenses could not make it out. As for the other pratenses, those belonging to the mixed community, they avoided their sometime sisters, would not fight with them, but carried the pupae into the nest. The hostility was all on the side of the newcomers. Next day some of them had been admitted as members of the mixed community, and ere long relations were permanently established on a peace footing. Not in a single instance did the pratenses of the mixed community join with the newcomers to attack the sanguineae. The alliance between pratenses and sanguineae was stronger than the racial brotherhood of the pratenses; the enmity between the two hostile species had been permanently overcome.[82]

*

* *

Such examples suffice to show how grave is the mistake of those who believe that instincts are quasi-sacred, and who, after they have included the fighting instinct in this category, regard it as imposed by fate upon all living animals from the lowest to the highest. For, in the first place, instinct varies greatly in its cogency. We find it to be non-modifiable or modifiable, absolute or relative, permanent or transient, not merely as we pass from one genus to another, but within the same genus as we pass from species to species,[83] and within the same species as we pass from group to group. Instinct is not a starting point, but is itself a product of evolution. Like evolution in general, it is progressive. The most ingrained instinct is merely an instinct of great antiquity. The observations quoted above suffice to show that the war-making instinct is less ingrained, less primitive, than people are apt to suppose, for even among the most combative species of ants, it can be resisted, modified, and restrained. If these humble insects are able to react against it, if they can modify their natures, if they can replace wars of conquest by peaceful cooperation, if they can substitute allied states (or, yet more remarkable, mixed and united states) for enemy states—should man be willing to avow himself more enslaved than they by his worst instincts, and less able than they to master these instincts? It is sometimes said that war lowers us to the level of beasts. War reduces us below that level, if we show ourselves less capable of freeing ourselves from the fighting spirit than are certain animal societies. It would be rather humiliating to be compelled to admit their superiority. Chi lo sa?... For my part I am far from certain that man is, as he is said to be, the lord of creation; more often, man is the destructive tyrant. I am sure that in many things he could learn wisdom from these animal societies, older than his own and infinitely diversified.

I do not propose to prophesy whether humanity will succeed (any more than the ant communities) in gaining the mastery over blind instinct. But what strikes me, as I read Auguste Forel, is the conviction that no more in man than in the ants is such a victory radically impossible. To recognize that a particular advance is not impracticable even though we should fail to realise that advance, seems to me more encouraging than the belief that, whatever we attempt, we shall run our heads against a stone wall. The window is closed. It is thick with grime. Perhaps we shall never be able to open it. But between us and the sunlit air there is nothing but a pane of glass, which we can break if we will.[84]

June 1, 1918.

"Revue Mensuelle," Geneva, August, 1918.

XXII

ON BEHALF OF THE INTERNATIONAL OF THE MIND

This chapter relates to the plan for an Institute of the Nations, suggested by Gerhard Gran, professor at the University of Christiania, writing in the "Revue Politique Internationale" of Lausanne. My reply was first published in the same periodical, under the title "Pour une culture universelle" (On behalf of a universal civilisation).

GERHARD GRAN'S broad-minded appeal cannot fail to arouse echoes. I have read it with lively sympathy. He displays the virtue of modesty, so rare in our day. At a time when all the nations are making an arrogant parade of a superior mission of order or justice, organisation or liberty, a mission which authorises them to impose on other nations their own hallowed individuality (for each looks upon itself as the chosen people), we draw a breath of relief when we hear one of them, by the voice of Gerhard Gran, speaking not of its rights, but of its "debts." How noble, too, are his tones of frankness and gratitude!

"Among all the nations, ours is perhaps the one which has the greatest duty to perform, for our nation owes most to the others. What we have gained from international science is incalculable.... Our debts are manifest in all directions.... When we draw up our scientific balance-sheet in account with the rest of the world, the credit side is meagre. In this respect we have to speak chiefly of our passive advantages, and our modesty forbids us to refer to our active contributions."

How refreshing is such modesty! How refreshing is it in this world-crisis of delirious vanity! Nevertheless Ibsen's fellow-countrymen are entitled to hold their heads high among their European brethren; for more than any other writer the great Norwegian recluse has stamped with his seal both the drama and modern thought. The eyes of Young France turned towards him; the writer of these lines asked counsel of him.

All the nations are debtors one to another. Let us pool our debts and our possessions.

If there are any to-day for whom modesty is befitting, it is the intellectuals. The part they have played in this war has been abominable, unpardonable. Not merely did they do nothing to lessen the mutual lack of understanding, to limit the spread of hatred; with rare exceptions, they did everything in their power to disseminate hatred and to envenom it. To a considerable extent, this war was their war. Thousands of brains were poisoned by their murderous ideologies. Overweeningly self-confident, proud, implacable, they sacrificed millions of young lives to the triumph of the phantoms of their imagination. History will not forget.

Gerhard Gran expresses the fear that personal cooperation between intellectuals of the belligerent lands may prove impossible for many years. If he is thinking of the generation of those who are over fifty, of those who stayed at home and waged a war of words in the learned societies, the universities, and the editorial offices, I fancy that the Norwegian writer is not mistaken. There is little chance that these intellectuals will ever join hands. I should say that none of them will do so, were I not familiar with the brain's astounding faculty for forgetting, were I not familiar with this pitiful and yet salutary weakness, by which the mind is not deceived, but which is essential to its continued existence. But in the present case, oblivion will be difficult. The intellectuals have burned their boats. At the outset of the war it was still possible to hope that some of those who had been carried away by the blind passion of the opening days, would be able within a few months frankly to admit their mistake. They would not do so. Not one of them has done so on either side of the frontier. It was even possible to note that in proportion as the disastrous consequences to European civilisation became apparent, those whose mission it was to act as guardians of that civilisation, those upon whose shoulders part of the responsibility weighed, instead of admitting their mistake, did all they could to increase their own infatuation. How, then, can we hope, when the war is over, and when the disasters to which it will have led will have become unmistakable, that the intellectuals will curb their pride and will constrain themselves to say, "We were wrong"?—To ask this would be to ask too much. The older generation, I fear, will have to endure to the last its sickness of mind and its obstinacy. On this side there is little hope. We can only wait until the older generation has died out.

Those who wish to reknit the relations among the peoples, must turn their hopes towards the other generation, that of those who bleed in the armies. May they be preserved! They have been ruthlessly thinned out by the sickle of war. They might even be annihilated if the war should be prolonged and extended, as may happen, for all things are possible. Mankind stands, like Hercules, at the parting of the ways. One of these ways leads (if Asia takes a hand in the game, and accentuates yet further the characteristics of hideous destruction in which Germany has set an example inevitably followed by the other combatants) to the suicide of Europe.—But at the present hour we have still the right to hope that the young men of Europe, now enrolled in the armies, will survive in sufficient numbers to fulfil the mission that will devolve on them after the war, the mission of reconciling the thoughts of the enemy nations. In either camp, I know a number of independent spirits, who look forward, when peace is signed, to realising this intellectual communion. They propose to except from this communion none but those who, be it in their own or be it in the other camp, have prostituted thought to the work of hatred. When I reflect on these young men, I am firmly convinced (and herein I differ from Gerhard Gran) that after the war the minds of all lands will inter-penetrate one another far more effectively than they have ever done before. The nations which knew nothing of one another, or which saw one another only in the form of contemptuous caricatures, have learned during the last four years, in the mud of the trenches, and at grips with death, that they are the same suffering flesh. All are enduring the same ordeal, and in it they become brothers. This sentiment continues to grow. For when we attempt to foresee the changes which, after the war, will occur in the relationships between the nations, we do not sufficiently realise the extent to which the war will lead to other upheavals, which may well modify the very essence of the nations. Whatever may be the immediate upshot of happenings in Russia, the example of the New Russia will not fail to have its influence upon the other peoples. An intimate unity is becoming established in the soul of the peoples. It is as if they were connected by gigantic roots, spreading underground regardless of frontiers.—As for the intellectuals who, sitting apart from the common people, are not directly swept along by this social current, they none the less feel its influence by intuition and sympathy. Notwithstanding the efforts which, during these four years, have been made to break off all contact between the writers in the two camps, I know that in both, on the morrow of the peace, international magazines and other publications will be founded. I have first-hand information concerning such schemes, initiated by young writers, soldiers at the front, men permeated with the European spirit. Among those of my own generation, there are a few who will give wholehearted assistance to their younger brethren. In our view, we shall in this way serve, not merely the cause of mankind, but the cause of our own land, far better than that cause will be served by the evil counsellors who preach armed isolation. Every country which shuts itself apart pronounces its own death-sentence. Gone for ever are the days when the young and tumultuous energies of the European nations needed, for their clarification, to be surrounded by partition walls.—Let me quote a few words uttered by Jean Christophe in his riper age:

"I neither admire nor dread the nationalism of the present time. It will pass away with the present time; it is passing, it has already passed. It is but a rung in the ladder. Climb to the top.... Every nation felt [before the war] the imperious necessity of gathering its forces and making up its balance-sheet. For the last hundred years all the nations have been transformed by their mutual intercourse and the immense contributions of all the brains of the universe, building up new morality, new knowledge, new faith. Every man must examine his conscience, and know exactly what he is and what he has, before he can enter with the rest into the new age. A new age is coming. Humanity is on the point of signing a new lease of life. Society is on the point of springing into vigour with new laws. It is Sunday to-morrow. We are all balancing our accounts for the week, setting our houses in order, making them clean and tidy, so that, joining together, we may go into the presence of our common God and enter into a new covenant with Him."

The war will prove (even against our will) to have been the anvil upon which will have been forged the unity of the European soul.

It is my hope that this intellectual communion will not be restricted to the European peninsula, but will extend to Asia, to the two

Americas, and to the great islets of civilisation spread over the rest of the globe. It is absurd that the nations of western Europe should pride themselves upon the discovery of profound differences, at the very time when they have never resembled one another more closely in merits and defects; at a time when their thought and their literature are least notable for distinctive characteristics; when everywhere there becomes sensible a monotonous levelling of intelligence; when on all hands we discern individualities that are dishevelled, threadbare, limp. I will venture to say that all of them, with their united efforts, are incompetent to give us the hope of that mental renovation to which the world is entitled after this formidable convulsion. We must go to Russia, which has doors thrown wide open towards the eastern world, for there only will our faces be freshened by the new currents which are blowing in every department of thought.

Let us widen the concept of humanism, dear to our forefathers, though its meaning has been narrowed down to the signification of Greek and Latin manuals. In every age, states, universities, academies, all the conservative forces of the mind, have endeavoured to make humanism in this narrower sense a dike against the onslaughts of the new spirit, in philosophy, in morals, in aesthetics. The dike has burst. The framework of a privileged culture has been broken. To-day we have to accept humanism in its widest signification, embracing all the spiritual forces of the whole world. What we need is, panhumanism.

*

* *

It is our hope that this ideal, formulated here and there by a few leading minds, or heralded by the foundation while the war is yet in progress of centres for the study of universal civilisation,[85] shall be boldly adopted as its ensign by the international academy, in the foundation of which I hope (with Gerhard Gran) that Norway will take the initiative.

I note that Gerhard Gran seems, like Professor Fredrik Stang, to limit his ambitions to the foundation of an institute for scientific research, for in his view science is in its essence more international than art and letters. He writes:

"In art and literature we may, in case of need, discuss the advantages and disadvantages resulting from the isolation of one nation from the rest, or from the antagonism of human groups. In science, such a discussion is absurd. The kingdom of science is the whole world.... The atmosphere indispensable to science has nothing whatever to do with national conflicts."

I think that this distinction is not so well founded as it may seem. No domain of mental activity has been more disastrously involved in the war than the domain of science. Whereas art and letters have only too often been accessory stimulants of the crime, science furnished the war with its weapons, did its utmost to render them more atrocious, to widen the bounds of suffering and cruelty. I may add that even in time of peace I have always been struck by the bitterness of national sentiment displayed by men of science. Those of every nation are fond of accusing their foreign colleagues of stealing their best discoveries and forgetting to acknowledge the source. In a word, science shares in the evil passions which corrode art and letters.

On the other hand, if science needs the collaboration of all the nations, to art and letters to-day it is no less advantageous that they should abandon a position of "splendid isolation." Without speaking of the technical advances which, in painting and music, have during the course of the nineteenth century and of the one which has begun so badly brought such sudden and enormous enrichment to the aesthetics of sight and hearing—apart from such considerations—the influence of one philosopher, one thinker, one writer, can modify the whole literature of an epoch, switching the mind on to a new road in psychological, moral, aesthetic, or social research. If any one wish to be isolated, isolated let him be! But the republic of the mind tends to enlarge its frontiers day by day. The greatest men are those who know how to embrace and fuse in a single vigorous personality the wealth that is dispersed or latent in the soul of all mankind.

Let us refrain, therefore, from limiting the idea of internationalism to the field of science. Let us give the fullest possible amplitude to the scheme. Let us form a world-wide Institute of Art, Letters and Science.

*

* *

Moreover, I do not think that this foundation could continue isolated. No longer, to-day, can the internationalism of culture remain the luxury of a few privileged persons. The practical value of an Institute of Nations would be small, unless the masters were associated with their disciples in the same stream, unless all the levels of culture were permeated with the same spirit.

That is why I greet, as a fruitful initiative and a happy symptom, the recent foundation in Zurich, by the university students of that city, of an International Association of Students (Internationaler Studentenbund). Let me quote from its program.

"Painfully affected by the great ordeal of the war, academic youth has realised the peculiar social responsibilities enjoined by the privileges of a studious life, and desires to find a remedy for the deeper causes of the evil.... The Association will endeavour to bring together those of all countries who are in close touch with university life, to unite them in a common faith in the advantages of the free development of the mind. It groups them for the struggle against the growing empery of mechanism and militarism in all the manifestations of life.... It hopes to realise the ideal of universities which shall remain centres of higher culture, in the service of truth alone, unsullied shrines of scientific research, absolutely independent in matters of opinion, paying no attention to selfish aims or to class interests."

This demand for the freedom of scientific research and for independence of thought, this organisation of young intellectuals for the defence of a right so essential and hitherto so incessantly violated, seem to me matters of primary necessity. If you desire that the cooperation between the teachers in different countries should not remain purely speculative, it is not enough that the teachers should associate their efforts. It is further essential that their thoughts shall be able to spread freely and to fructify in the minds of the young intellectuals throughout the world. Let us have no more of these barriers erected by the states between the two classes, between the two ages, of those who are engaged in the search for truth—teachers and students.

*

* *

My dream goes further. I should like the seed of universal culture to be scattered, from the very beginning of education, among the pupils of the primary and secondary schools. Above all let me suggest that throughout the countries of Europe an international language should be one of the compulsory subjects of study. Such international languages (Esperanto, Ido) have already attained something very near perfection; and with the minimum of effort the international language could be mastered by all the children of the civilised world. Not merely would this language be of unrivalled practical value throughout life. It would further serve as an introduction to the study of foreign languages and of their own national tongue; for it would make them realise, far better than any express instruction, the common elements in the European languages and the unity of European thought.

I would further insist that both in primary and secondary education there should be given a sketch of the history of universal thought, universal literature, universal art. I consider it utterly erroneous that the syllabus of instruction should concern itself only with these subjects as manifested within the limits of a single nation, and that within those limits there should be a further restriction to a period of two or three centuries. Despite all that has been done to modernise education, its spirit still remains essentially archaic. It perpetuates among us the atmosphere of extinct epochs. Let not this criticism be misunderstood. All my own education was classical. I passed through every stage of university instruction. In my student days we were still taught to write Latin speeches and Latin verses. I am impregnated with the ideas of classical art and classical thought. Far from desiring to sweep these things away, I should wish such treasures, like those of our Louvre, to be made accessible to the great mass of mankind. But I must point out that we should remain free in relation to that which we admire, and that we are not free in relation to classical thought. The Greco-Roman mental formulas, which our education has made as it were second nature, are nowise suited for application to modern problems. Those into whose minds such formulas have been instilled in childhood have acquired overwhelming prejudices which they are rarely, if ever, able to shake off, prejudices which weigh heavily upon contemporary society. I am inclined to believe that one of the moral errors from which Europe is chiefly suffering to-day, the Europe whose members are tearing one another to pieces, is that we have preserved the heroic and rhetorical idol of the Greco-Roman fatherland, which corresponds no better to the natural sentiment of the fatherland to-day than the deities of Homer correspond to the true religious needs of our time.

Humanity grows older, but does not ripen. It is still enmeshed in the teachings of childhood. Its greatest fault is its slothful unwillingness to seek renewal. But humanity must seek renewal and growth. For centuries it has condemned itself to use no more than a modicum of its spiritual resources. It is like a half-paralysed colossus. It allows some of its organs to atrophy. Are we not weary of these infirm nations, of these scattered members of a great body, which might dominate our planet!

Membra sumus corporis magni.

Let these members unite; let Humanity, the New Adam, arise!

VILLENEUVE, *March 15, 1918.*

"Revue Politique Internationale," Lausanne, March and April, 1918.

XXIII

A CALL TO EUROPEANS

IN the downfall of imperial Germany, there stand out the great names of a few free spirits of Germany, the names of those who during the last four years have strenuously defended the rights of conscience and reason against the abuses of force. The name of G. F. Nicolai is one of the most illustrious among these. I devoted two articles[86] to the study of his excellent work, *The Biology of War*, and have recorded the conditions under which it was written. This distinguished professor of physiology at the university of Berlin, a celebrated physician, appointed at the outbreak of the war as chief of one of the army medical departments, was cashiered because he had expressed his disapproval of the misdeeds committed by the statesmen and the high military commanders of Germany. Suffering humiliation after humiliation, degraded to the rank of private, sentenced to five months' imprisonment by the Danzig court-martial, he at length fled from Germany in order to escape yet severer punishment. A few months ago we learned from the newspapers of his daring escape in an aeroplane. He has secured asylum in Denmark, and in that country he has just published the first number of a review, to whose historical and human interest I now wish to call attention.

*

* *

This periodical is entitled "Das werdende Europa,—Blätter für zukunftsfrohe Menschen,—neutral gegenüber den kriegführenden Ländern,—leidenschaftlich Partei ergreifend für das Recht gegen die Macht." (The Coming Europe,—a review for men who look joyously towards the future,—neutral as regards the belligerent lands,—but taking sides passionately on behalf of right against might.)[87]

Looking joyously towards the future! This is one of Nicolai's most salient characteristics, and I have alluded to it at the close of my critique of his *Biology of War*. How many in his place would have been disheartened by all that he has seen, heard, and endured in the way of human malice; of cowardice, which is worse; and of folly, which is yet more intolerable—the folly that rules the world! But Nicolai is a man of extraordinary elasticity. "Nicht weinen!" as his little girl of two says to him when he is about to leave her and everything he loves. "Not cry!" Looking joyously towards the future. To uphold him in this joyance he has his wonderful vitality, the inviolable strength of his convictions, his triumphant assurance (meine triumphierende Sicherheit). He displays an apostolic zeal which we should hardly have expected in a scientific observer; but

Nicolai, of a sudden, becomes from time to time a seer, an idealist, a prophet, like the religious heroes of old. With all his equipment of modern science, he is a strange instance of reincarnation. The Old Germany of Goethe, Herder, and Kant, speaks to us through his voice. To use his own words, he claims his rights as against the right of Ludendorff and other usurpers to adopt the political methods of the Tatars.

The aim of "Coming Europe" is, he tells us, to "awaken love for our new, our greater fatherland, Europe.... We wish that all the peoples of Europe shall become useful and happy members of this new organism."—Now the future of Europe mainly depends upon the condition of Germany, a country which, by its brutal disregard of European principles, supports the old policy of armed isolation. The primary aim, therefore, must be the liberation of Germany.

The first issue of the magazine contains an inaugural article by Professor Kristoffer Nyrop, member of the Royal Academy of Denmark. It further includes interesting pages written by Dr. Alfred H. Fried, and by Carl Lindhagen, burgomaster of Stockholm. But the main contribution, filling three-fourths of the number, is a long article by Nicolai, entitled "Warum ich aus Deutschland ging. Offener Brief an denjenigen Unbekannten, der die Macht hat in Deutschland."[88] These words are the confession of a great spirit, of one whom the oppressors have wished to enslave, but who has broken his chains.

Nicolai opens by explaining what has led him to an act which has cost him dear, the abandonment of his country in the hour of danger. In touching terms he expresses his love for the motherland (which he contrasts with Europe, his fatherland), his love for Germany and for all that he owes it. He tore himself away only because there was no other means of working for the liberation of his country. While he remained in Germany, he could do nothing; for years of tribulation had been the proof. Right was shackled. Germany was no longer a Rechtsstaat. Oppression was universal; and, still worse, it was anonymous. The power of the sword, irresponsible, was supreme. Parliament no longer existed. The press no longer existed. The chancellor, the emperor himself, were subject to the mysterious

"Unknown who rules Germany." Nicolai tells us that he had long waited for others better qualified than himself to speak. He had waited in vain. Fear, corruption, lack of determination, stifled all attempts at revolt. The soul of Germany was dumb.—Even he, Nicolai, would perhaps have held his peace to the end, constrained to silence by the sentiment of chivalrous loyalty which influences everyone in time of war, had he not been driven to extremities, had he not been brought to bay, by the unknown power. After everything had been taken from him, after he had been despoiled of his honours, of his official position, of the comforts and even the necessaries of life, those in authority wished to wrest from him the one thing that still remained, his right to obey, his convictions. This was too much, and he fled. "I was compelled to leave the German empire; I left, because I believe myself to be a good German."

To enable us to understand his decision, he describes for us the four years of daily struggle which had been his lot in Germany before he made up his mind to leave.—Notwithstanding his views on the war, when it actually broke out he put himself at the disposal of the military authorities, but only as a civilian medical man (vertraglich verpflichteter Zivilarzt). He was appointed principal medical officer in the new Tempelhof hospital, a post which permitted him to continue his public lectures at the university of Berlin. But in October, 1914, in conjunction with Professor W. Foerster, Professor A. Einstein, and Dr. Buek, he issued a protest, couched in very strong terms, against the notorious manifesto of the 93. Punishment did not tarry. He was at once relieved of his post, and was appointed medical assistant at the isolation hospital in the little fortress of Graudenz. Being under no illusions as to the reasons for this arbitrary and absurd measure, he devoted his spare time to the preparation of his book, *The Biology of War*. Now came the sinking of the Lusitania, which was a terrible shock to Nicolai, affecting him as if he had been struck with a whip. At dinner with a few of his comrades, he declared that the violation of Belgian neutrality, the use of poison gas, and the torpedoing of merchantmen, were not merely immoral actions, but were acts of incredible stupidity, which would sooner or later ruin the German empire. One of those present, his colleague Dr. Knoll, could find nothing better to do than to inform against him. Anew dismissed from his post, Nicolai was sent in disgrace to one of the most out-of-the-way corners of Germany. He protested in the name of justice. He appealed to the emperor. The latter, he was given to understand, wrote on the margin of the report of his case: "Der Mann ist ein Idealist, man soll ihn gewähren lassen!" (The man is an idealist. Let him alone!)

He was sent back to Berlin in the winter of 1915-16, with instructions to be on his good behaviour. Ignoring these instructions, immediately after his return to the university he began a course of lectures upon "War as an evolutionary Factor in human History." The lectures were promptly prohibited, and Nicolai was sent to Danzig, where he was strictly forbidden to speak or write on political topics. Nicolai took exception to this order, on the ground that he was a civilian. Thereupon an attempt was made to administer to him the oath of loyalty and obedience. He refused. Summoned before a court-martial, and warned of the consequences of refusal, he persisted. He was thereupon reduced to the ranks, and for two and a half years was engaged in futile clerical work as a private in the army medical corps. Nevertheless, he finished his book, and it went to press in Germany. The first two hundred pages had been set up when an information against it was lodged by the chief clerk of a great submarine dockyard, who said indignantly, "We earn our money arduously in the war, and this fellow is writing in favour of peace!" Nicolai was arrested and his manuscript was seized. After a lengthy trial, he was sentenced to five months' imprisonment. The newspapers were forbidden to mention his name. The "Danziger Zeitung" was suspended for having published an account of the trial. His troubles began afresh immediately he came out of prison. The commandant of Eilenburg wished to force Nicolai to accept combatant service. Nicolai refused, and was given twenty-four hours to think the matter over. He thought of Socrates, and of the Greek philosopher's obedience to his country's laws, bad though they were. But he thought also of Luther, who fled to the Wartburg to finish his work. And Nicolai left that night. Not even yet, however, did he quit Germany, for he wished to make a last appeal to the justice of his country. He wrote to the minister for war, relating the infractions of law to which he had been exposed, and asking for protection against the arbitrary proceedings of the military authorities. While awaiting an answer, he took refuge with friends, first in Munich, then in

Grunewald near Berlin. But no answer was received. He had, therefore, to expatriate himself. We know how he crossed the frontier, "in an aeroplane, two miles above the earth amid clouds formed by bursting shrapnel."[89] At dawn after Saint John's night, he saw the distant gleam of the sea of freedom. He reached Copenhagen. For the last time he addressed himself to the German government, offering to return upon guarantees that his rights should be respected, and that he should be reinstated. After eight weeks, he was declared to be a deserter. A raid was made upon his house in Berlin, and upon the houses of some of his friends. His goods were sequestrated. A demand was made for his extradition, upon the charge of stealing an aeroplane.—Then it was that, resuming freedom of speech, Nicolai wrote his "Open Letter" to the "Unknown" despot.

*

* *

What particularly strikes me in this narrative is, in the first place, the man's invincible tenacity, the way in which he stands upon his right as upon a fortress—"eine feste Burg." ...But I am also greatly impressed by the secret aid which was furnished him by so many of his compatriots.

People are astonished to-day at the sudden collapse of the German colossus. A hundred different reasons are given. We are told that the army is ravaged by epidemic disease; that the morale of the Germans has been undermined by bolshevist propaganda; and so on. These influences have played their part. But another cause has been forgotten. It is that the entire edifice, despite its imposing front, has been mined. Behind the façade of passive obedience, widespread disillusionment prevails. Nothing is more striking in Nicolai's story (notwithstanding all his precautions lest anything he may say should betray his friends to the vengeance of the authorities) than the way in which he has again and again been supported and encouraged by the devotion or by the tacit complicity of those with whom he came into contact. "Men of science, working men, rankers, and officers," he writes, "begged me to say what they did not dare to utter themselves." When he was arrested and when his book was seized, the manuscript was rescued and was smuggled into Switzerland. By whom? By an official German courier!—When, having fled from his post, he wished to leave Germany, and when, in the first instance, he thought of getting out of the country on foot, he was arrested a hundred yards short of the frontier and was taken before an elderly captain. "When he asked me my name, and I said, 'I am Professor Nicolai,' he looked at me long and quizzically. I am doubtful whether he knew that I was being hunted, but I have the impression that he did know.... He advised me, in friendly fashion, not again to attempt crossing the frontier by night, for the frontier patrols were accompanied by bloodhounds—then he let me go."—Seeing no other way of escape than by the air route, Nicolai turned—to whom? To an officer in the flying corps, asking the loan of an aeroplane, for a journey to Holland or Switzerland. The officer, without turning a hair, replied that the thing could be done, and that if Nicolai should decide to make his way to Denmark (which would be much easier) they could start with a whole air-squadron. In the end, as we know, there was no squadron; but two aeroplanes and a number of officers participated in the flight from Neurippin to Copenhagen.—Many similar incidents, though perhaps less striking than those quoted, serve to show the dissolution of the bonds between the citizens and the state. The publication of Nicolai's book in Switzerland, and the subsequent clandestine circulation in Germany of one hundred copies, brought him into relationships with persons belonging to all parties in Germany, and enabled him to realise how deep and passionate was the feeling of hatred diffused throughout all strata of the population. He adds: "I am convinced that Germany and the world would be liberated to-morrow, if only all the Germans were to say to-day without reserve that which, at the bottom of their hearts, they wish and ardently desire."

Herein lies the force of his protest. It is not the protest of one individual, but that of an entire nation. Nicolai is merely the spokesman.

Thus, having told his tale, he turns to the people, he turns to those who inspired him to speak. By a sudden transformation, the "Unknown" to whom he addresses his "Open Letter"—derjenige Unbekannte, der die Macht hat—is no longer the military authority.

Sovereign power seems already to have passed into the hands of the real master, the German people. He invites the German people to enter into a union with the other peoples. In the tone of an inspired evangelist, he reminds the German people of its true destiny, its spiritual mission, a thousandfold more important than any empty victory. To all the peoples of Europe, he points out the duty of the hour, the pressing task: to achieve the unity of Europe and the organisation of the world.

"Come, then, kindred spirits!... I am a free man, freed from everything in the world, free from the state [staatenlos], ein deutscher Weltbürger [a German citizen of the world].... I have peace! [Ich habe Frieden].... Come! Cry aloud what you already know and feel!... We do not wish to *make* peace; we simply wish to realise that we *have* peace...."

Reiterating his cry of October, 1914, the Call to Europeans[90] which he, in conjunction with his friends Albert Einstein, Wilhelm Foerster, and Otto Buek, issued as a counterblast to the insane utterances of the 93, he reaffirms his act of faith in the spirit of Europe, one and brotherly; and he launches his appeal to all the free spirits, to those whom Goethe long ago termed: "Good Europeans."

October 20, 1918.

"Wissen und Leben," Zurich, November, 1918.

XXIV

OPEN LETTER TO PRESIDENT WILSON

MONSIEUR LE PRÉSIDENT,

THE peoples are breaking their chains. The hour foreseen by you and desired by you is at hand. May it not come in vain! From one end of Europe to the other, there is rising among the peoples the will to resume control of their destinies, and to unite, that they may form a regenerated Europe. Across the frontiers, they are holding out their hands to one another for a friendly clasp. But between them there still remain abysses of mistrust and misunderstanding. These abysses must be bridged. We must break the fetters of ancient destiny which shackle these peoples to nationalist wars; which have compelled them, century after century, to rush blindly upon one another for their mutual destruction. Unaided, they cannot break their chains. They are calling for help. But whither can they turn for help?

You alone, Monsieur le Président, among all those whose dread duty it now is to guide the policy of the nations, you alone enjoy a world-wide moral authority. You inspire universal confidence. Answer the appeal of these passionate hopes! Take the hands which are stretched forth, help them to clasp one another. Help these peoples, groping in the dark, to find their way, to establish the new charter of freedom and union whose principles they are seeking earnestly but confusedly.

Reflect: Europe is in danger of falling back into the circles of hell through which she has been toiling for more than four years, drenching the soil with her blood. In all lands, the peoples have lost confidence in the ruling classes. At this hour, you are the only one who can speak to all alike—to the common people and to the bourgeoisies of the nations. You alone can be sure of an attentive hearing. None but you can act as mediator to-day (and will even you still be able to act as mediator to-morrow?). Should this mediator fail to appear, the human masses, disarrayed and unbalanced, will almost inevitably break forth into excesses. The common people will welter in bloody chaos, while the parties of traditional order will fly to bloody reaction. Class wars, racial wars, wars between the nations of yesterday, wars between the nations which have just been formed, blind social convulsions, with no further aim than the gratification of the hatreds, the envies, the crazy dreams of an hour of life looking forward to no morrow....

Heir of George Washington and Abraham Lincoln, take up the cause, not of a party, not of a single people, but of all! Summon the representatives of the peoples to the Congress of Mankind! Preside over it with the full authority which you hold in virtue of your lofty moral consciousness and in virtue of the great future of America! Speak, speak to all! The world hungers for a voice which will overleap the frontiers of nations and of classes. Be the arbiter of the free peoples! Thus may the future hail you by the name of Reconciler!

ROMAIN ROLLAND.

VILLENEUVE, *November 9, 1918.*

"Le Populaire," Paris, November 18, 1918.

*

* *

A few days later (December 4, 1918), "Le Populaire" published a letter from Romain Rolland to Jean Longuet, wherein Romain Rolland laid bare his most intimate thought and gave the reasons for his attitude towards Wilson. The letter was reprinted by "L'Humanité" in the issue of December 14, 1918, a special "Wilson Number."

I am no Wilsonian. I see all too plainly that the president's message, as clever as it is generous, aims (in good faith) at realising throughout the world the ideal of the bourgeois republic of the Franco-American type.

This is a conservative ideal and it no longer satisfies me.

Nevertheless, despite our personal predilections and our reserves for the future, I believe that the best thing we can do for the moment is to support the action of President Wilson. He alone will be able to curb the greedy appetites, the ambitions, and the fierce instincts, which will seat themselves at the peace banquet. Through his action alone is there any chance of bringing about a modus vivendi in Europe, one which provisionally at least shall be fairly just. This great bourgeois embodies what is purest, most disinterested, most humane, in the mentality of his class.[91] No one is better fitted than he to act as Arbiter.

R. R.

June, 1919.

XXV

AGAINST VICTORIOUS BISMARCKISM

"Le Populaire" asked Romain Rolland to write an article on the occasion of President Wilson's arrival in France. Romain Rolland, who was ill at the time, wrote from Villeneuve as follows.

THURSDAY, *December 12, 1918.*

DEAR LONGUET,

YOUR letter of the 6th inst. did not reach me until to-day, of course after being opened by the military censorship. It finds me in bed, where I have been for a fortnight, suffering from an obstinate attack of influenza. It is therefore impossible for me to write the article you want.

All that I will say is that, during the last fortnight, the news from France has often made me more uneasy than my fever. The Allies believe themselves victorious. In my view (if they fail to pull themselves together) they are vanquished, beaten, infected, by Bismarckism.

Unless there is an extensive turn in events, I foresee a century of hatreds, of new wars of revenge, and the destruction of European civilisation. Let me add that the destruction of European civilisation is hardly to be regretted if the victorious nations prove thus incapable of guiding their destinies.

It is my hope that, amid the intoxicating but deceptive triumphs of the present, they may regain the consciousness of their crushing responsibilities towards the future! It is my hope that they will remember that every one of their mistakes or their sins of omission will have to be paid for by their children and their children's children!

Excuse these lines, scribbled by a convalescent, and believe me, my dear Longuet,

Yours as always,
ROMAIN ROLLAND.

"Le Populaire," Paris, December 21, 1918.

XXVI

DECLARATION OF THE INDEPENDENCE OF THE MIND

BRAIN workers, comrades, scattered throughout the world, kept apart for five years by the armies, the censorship and the mutual hatred of the warring nations, now that barriers are falling and frontiers are being reopened, we issue to you a call to reconstitute our brotherly union, but to make of it a new union more firmly founded and more strongly built than that which previously existed.

The war has disordered our ranks. Most of the intellectuals placed their science, their art, their reason, at the service of the governments. We do not wish to formulate any accusations, to launch any reproaches. We know the weakness of the individual mind and the elemental strength of great collective currents. The latter, in a moment, swept the former away, for nothing had been prepared to help in the work of resistance. Let this experience, at least, be a lesson to us for the future!

First of all, let us point out the disasters that have resulted from the almost complete abdication of intelligence throughout the world, and from its voluntary enslavement to the unchained forces. Thinkers, artists, have added an incalculable quantity of envenomed hate to the plague which devours the flesh and the spirit of Europe. In the arsenal of their knowledge, their memory, their imagination, they have sought reasons for hatred, reasons old and new, reasons historical, scientific, logical, and poetical. They have worked to destroy mutual understanding and mutual love among men. So doing, they have disfigured, defiled, debased, degraded Thought, of which they were the representatives. They have made it an instrument of the passions; and (unwittingly, perchance) they have made it a tool of the selfish interests of a political or social clique, of a state, a country, or a class. Now, when, from the fierce conflict in which the nations have been at grips, the victors and the vanquished emerge equally stricken, impoverished, and at the bottom of their hearts (though they will not admit it) utterly ashamed of their access of mania—now, Thought, which has been entangled in their struggles, emerges, like them, fallen from her high estate.

Arise! Let us free the mind from these compromises, from these unworthy alliances, from these veiled slaveries! Mind is no one's servitor. It is we who are the servitors of mind. We have no other master. We exist to bear its light, to defend its light, to rally round it all the strayed sheep of mankind. Our role, our duty, is to be a centre of stability, to point out the pole star, amid the whirlwind of passions in the night. Among these passions of pride and mutual destruction, we make no choice; we reject them all. Truth only do we honour; truth that is free, frontierless, limitless; truth that knows nought of the prejudices of race or caste. Not that we lack interest in humanity. For humanity we work, but for humanity as a whole. We know nothing of peoples. We know the People, unique and universal; the People which suffers, which struggles, which falls and rises to its feet once more, and which continues to advance along the rough road drenched with its sweat and its blood; the People, all men, all alike our brothers. In order that they may, like ourselves, realise this brotherhood, we raise above their blind struggles the Ark of the Covenant—Mind which is free, one and manifold, eternal.

R. R.

VILLENEUVE, *Spring, 1919.*

[This manifesto was published in "L'Humanité," June 26, 1919.]

By the end of 1919, the following signatures had been received to the above declaration.

- Addams, Jane (U.S.A.).
- Alain [Chartier] (France).
- Alexandre, Raoul (on the staff of "L'Humanité," France).
- Arco, G. von (Germany).
- Arcos, René (France).
- Barbusse, Henri (France).
- Baudouin, Charles (editor of "Le Carmel," France).
- Bazalgette, Léon (France).
- Bernaert, Edouard (France).
- Besnard, Lucien (France).
- Bignami, Enrico (editor of "Coenobium," Italy).
- Biriukov, Paul (Russia).

- Bloch, Ernest (Switzerland).
- Bloch, Jean-Richard (France).
- Bodin, Louise (editor of "La Voix des Femmes," France).
- Bracco, Roberto (Italy).
- Brooks, Van Wyck (U.S.A.).
- Brouwer, L. J. (Holland).
- Buchet, Samuel (France).
- Burnet, E. (of the Pasteur Institute, France).
- Carpenter, Edward (England).
- Chateaubriant, A. de (France).
- Chenevière, Georges (France).
- Colin, Paul (editor of "L'Art Libre," Belgium).
- Coomaraswamy, Ananda (Hindustan).
- Costa, Benedicto (Brazil).
- Croce, Benedetto (Italy).
- Crucy, François (on the staff of "L'Humanité," France).
- Desanges, Paul (on the staff of "La Forge," France).
- Desprès, Fernand (France).
- Dickinson, G. Lowes (England).
- Donvalis, Georges (Greece).
- Doyen, Albert (France).
- Duhamel, Georges (France).
- Dujardin, Edouard (editor of "Cahiers Idéalistes," France).
- Dunois, Amédée (on the staff of "L'Humanité, France).
- Dupin, Gustave (France).
- Dy, Melot du (Belgium).
- Eder, Robert (Switzerland).
- Eeckhoud, Georges (Belgium).
- Eeden, Frederick van (Holland).
- Einstein, Albert (Germany).
- Eslander, J. F. (Belgium).
- Fiévez, Joseph (France).
- Foerster, W. (Germany).
- Forel, Auguste (Switzerland).
- Frank, Leonhard (Germany).
- Frank, Waldo (U.S.A.).
- Fried, A. H. (German-Austria).
- Fry, R. (England).

- George, Waldemar (on the staff of "La Forge," France).
- Georges-Bazille, G. (editor of "Cahiers Britanniques et
- Américains," France).
- Gerlach, H. von (Germany).
- Goll, Ivan (Germany).
- Hamon, Augustin (France).
- Heidenstam, Verner von (Sweden).
- Hellens, Franz (Belgium).
- Herzog, Wilhelm (Germany).
- Hesse, Hermann (Germany).
- Hier, Frederick P. (U.S.A.).
- Hilbert, David (Germany).
- Hofer, Charles (Switzerland).
- Holmes, John Haynes (U.S.A.).
- Huebsch, B. W. (U.S.A.).
- Jouve, P. J. (France).
- Kapteyn, J. C. (Holland).
- Key, Ellen (Sweden).
- Khnopff, Georges (Belgium).
- Kollwitz, Käte (Germany).
- Labouré, A. M. (France).
- Lagerlöf, Selma (Sweden).
- Laisant, C. A. (France).
- Latzko, Andreas (Hungary).
- Lefebvre, Raymond (France).
- Lehmann, Max (Germany).
- Lindhagen, Carl (Sweden).
- Liveright, Horace B. (U.S.A.).
- Lopez-Pico, M. (Spain).
- Lucci, Arnaldo (Italy).
- Mann, Heinrich (Germany).
- Martinet, Marcel (France).
- Maseras, Alfons (Spain).
- Masereel, Frans (Belgium).
- Masson, Émile (France).
- Masters, Edgar Lee (U.S.A.).
- Matisse, Georges (France).
- Matisse, Madeline (France).

- Mercereau, Alexandre (France).
- Mériga, Lue (editor of "La Forge," France).
- Mesnil, Jacques (Belgium).
- Michaelis, Sophus (Denmark).
- Moissi, A. (Germany).
- Morhardt, Mathias (France).
- Natorp, Paul (Germany).
- Nearing, Scott (U.S.A.).
- Nicolai, Georg Friedrich (Germany).
- Nithack-Stahn (Germany).
- Ors, Eugenio d' (Spain).
- Paasche, H. (Germany).
- Picard, Edmond (Belgium).
- Pierre, A. (on the staff of "L'Humanité," France).
- Prenant, A. (France).
- Ragaz (Switzerland).
- Reuillard, Gabriel (France).
- Rolland, Romain (France).
- Romains, Jules (France).
- Roorda van Eysinga, H. (Switzerland).
- Roussel, Nelly (France).
- Rubakin, Nicholas (Russia).
- Rusiecka, M. de (Poland).
- Russell, Bertrand (England).
- Ryner, Han (France).
- Schirardin, (professor in Metz, France).
- Schneider, Edouard (France).
- Schoen, Edouard (professor in Metz, France).
- Schultz, P. (professor in Metz, France).
- Sévérine (France).
- Signac, Paul (France).
- Sinclair, Upton (U.S.A.).
- Sorel, Robert (France).
- Stieglitz, Alfred (U.S.A.).
- Stocker, Helene (Germany).
- Suchenno, Jean (France).
- Tagore, Rabindranath (Hindustan).
- Thiessou, Gaston (France).

- Uhry, Jules (on the staff of "L'Humanité," France).
- Unruh, Fritz von (Germany).
- Vaillant-Couturier, Paul (France).
- Velde, Henry van de (Belgium).
- Vildrac, Charles (France).
- Villard, Oswald Garrison (U.S.A.).
- Viskovatov, L. de (Russia).
- Wacker (professor at Metz, France).
- Wehberg, H. (Germany).
- Werfel, Franz (Germany).
- Werth, Léon (France).
- Yannios (Greece).
- Zangwill, Israel (England).
- Zweig, Stefan (German-Austria).

Emilio H. del Villar, editor of "Archive Geografico de la Peninsula Iberica," of Madrid, has sent me a manifesto *Por la causa de la civilizacion*, published in the Madrid newspapers in June, 1919, and inspired with sentiments analogous to those of the above declaration. This manifesto is signed by about one hundred Spanish writers and men of science, university professors, etc. Emilio H. del Villar sends his own adhesion, together with that of all the signatories of the Spanish manifesto, to the Declaration of the Independence of the Mind.

It is a matter for regret that we have not been able to add to the list the signatures of our Russian friends from whom we are still cut off by the governmental blockade. We keep their places open. Russian thought is in the vanguard of the thought of the world.

R. R.

August, 1919.

SUPPLEMENTARY NOTE TO CHAPTER XX

A GREAT EUROPEAN: G. F. NICOLAI

COMMENT is requisite upon the reproaches addressed by G. F. Nicolai to certain Christian sects. In the various countries of Europe, opposition to the war, on the part of those he names, was far more vigorous than has been commonly supposed. Inasmuch as the authorities ruthlessly but silently suppressed all opposition, it is only since the close of the war that we have been able to glean information concerning these conscientious revolts and sacrifices. Without dwelling upon the story of the thousands of conscientious objectors in the United States and in England (where Bertrand Russell has been their defender and interpreter), I wish to mention that Paul Birinkov has drawn my attention to the attitude of the Nazarenes in Hungary and Serbia, where large numbers of them were shot. He has also given me information concerning the doings of the Tolstoyans, the Dukhobors, the Adventists, the Young Baptists, etc., in Russia. As for the Mennonites, according to the reports of Dr. Pierre Kennel, in the United States most of them refused to subscribe to the war loans. They were not compelled to undertake combatant duties, but they accepted service in the battalions for the reconstruction of the devastated regions in northern France. In tsarist Russia, and in a number of the German states, they were granted exemption from combatant service, and did duty in the medical corps or other auxiliary drafts. In France, by a decree of the Convention (respected by Napoleon) they were likewise assigned to non-combatant service. But the Third Republic disregarded this decree.

R. R.

Printed in Great Britain by UNWIN BROTHERS, LIMITED, THE GRESHAM PRESS, WOKING AND LONDON

FOOTNOTES:

[1] Published in pamphlet form by La Maison Française, Paris, 1918.

[2] Except the last two stanzas, which were composed in the autumn of the same year.

[3] Conversation with L. Mabilleau, "Opinion," June 20, 1908.

[4] In a recent issue of the "Revue des Deux Mondes."

[5] Institut für Kulturforschung (Institute for the Study of Civilisation), founded at Vienna in February, 1915, by Dr. Erwin Hanslick. So rapid was its success that in February, 1916, it gave birth to the Institute for the Study of the East and the Orient.

[6] "Nature," writes Voltaire in *L'Homme aux quarante écus,* "is like those great princes who think nothing of the loss of 400,000 men, provided they can fulfil their own august designs."

The princes of to-day, great and small alike, are more spendthrift!

[7] Cf. Victor Bérard's brief account of the Manchurian campaign in *La révolte de l'Asie*. Cf. also *Les derniers jours de Pékin,* where Pierre Loti describes the destruction of Tung-Chow, "the City of Celestial Purity."

[8] Numerous issues of "Cahiers de la Quinzaine" have been devoted to castigating the crimes of civilisation. I may mention:

- (*a*) Sur le Congo, by E. D. Morel, Pierre Mille, and Félicien Challaye
- ("Cahiers de la Quinzaine," vii, 6, 12, 16).
- (*b*) Sur les Juifs en Russie et en Roumanie, by Bernard Lazare, Elie
- Eberlin, and Georges Delahache (iii, 8; vi, 6).
- (*c*) Sur la Pologne, by Edmond Bernus (viii, 10, 12, 14).
- (*d*) Sur l'Arménie, by Pierre Quillard (iii, 19).
- (*e*) Sur la Finlande, by Jean Deck (iii, 21).

[9] Arnold Porret, *Les causes profondes de la guerre,* Lausanne, 1916.

[10] From a lecture entitled Nationalism in Japan, since republished in the volume *Nationalism,* Macmillan, London, 1917 (pp. 59 and 60). This address marks a turning-point in the history of the world.

[11] Consult a number of shrewd articles published during the last decade by Francis Delaisi. One in particular may be mentioned, that which appeared in "Pages libres" on January 1, 1907, dealing with foreign affairs in 1906 (the Algeciras year). He gives striking examples of what he terms "industrialised diplomacy." As a

complement to Delaisi, read the financial articles of the "Revue" (issues for November and December, 1906) signed Lysis, and the commentary on these articles by P. G. La Chesnais in "Pages libres" (January 19, 1907). In these writings we find a plain demonstration of the power of the financial oligarchies over the governments of the European states, alike republics and monarchies—a power that is "collective, mysterious in its workings, and independent of control."

[12] Let me quote a few lines from Maurras, so lucid a writer when not under the spell of his fixed idea. "The Money State governs, gilds, and decorates Intelligence: but muzzles it and puts it to sleep. The Money State, at will, can prevent Intelligence from becoming aware of a political truth; and if Intelligence utters a political truth, the Money State can prevent that truth from being heard and understood. How can a country realise its own needs if those who know them can be condemned to silence, to falsehood, or to isolation?" (L'Avenir de l'Intelligence.)—A true picture of the present day.

[13] Introduction to Marcelle Capy's book *Une voix de femme dans la mêlée,* Ollendorff, Paris, 1916. The italicised passages were suppressed by the censor in the original publication.

[14] On page 26 of Marcelle Capy's book we learn how touching a response these utterances of stalwart sympathy have called forth from the generous hearts of our soldiers.

[15] Published at Geneva by J. H. Jeheber, 1917; English translation *The Journal of Leo Tolstoi* (1895-1899), Knopf, New York, 1917.

[16] December 7, 1895.

[17] An exception must be made as regards certain voices from Germany, among which that of Professor Foerster speaks in the clearest tones. But we should err were we to allow ourselves to be persuaded that such unbiassed persons are a German monopoly, should we fail to realise that similar voices are raised in the other camp.

[18] This is shown by the recent establishment and the success of Swiss periodicals which embody a reaction against the tendencies

described in the text. Moreover, regrets similar to those voiced above have been repeatedly expressed by Swiss writers of independent mind. I may mention H. Hodler ("La Voix de L'Humanité"); E. Platzhoff-Lejeune ("Coenobium" and the "Revue mensuelle"); Adolphe Ferrière ("Coenobium" for March and April, 1917, in an article entitled The Effect of the Press and of the Censorship in Promoting Mutual Hatred among the Nations).

[19] "The Masses, a free magazine," 34 Union Square East, New York.—All the items in the text are quoted from the issues of June and July, 1917.

[20] Advertising Democracy, June, 1917, p. 5.

[21] Who wanted War, June, 1917, p. 23.

[22] Socialists and War, June, 1917, p. 25.

[23] The Religion of Patriotism, July, 1917.

[24] On Not Going to the War, July, 1917.

[25] Patriotism in the Middle West, June, 1917.

[26] This is said to have happened in the case of "Pearson's Magazine." (Consult the article on Free Speech, "The Masses," July, 1917.)—It is hardly necessary to refer to the masterly manner in which all independent persons who displease the authorities are implicated in imaginary plots.

[27] Issue of July, 1917.

[28] Since the article above quoted was published, the American Senate has imposed heavy taxation on war profits.

[29] E. D. Morel, having served his sentence, has given a number of lectures in various parts of Britain, arousing the sympathetic indignation of his audiences by his account of the illegalities in his trial and of the undercurrents in the whole business. He was able to show that there were influences at work emanating from certain persons whose interests had been injuriously affected prior to the

war by Morel's press campaign against the Congo atrocities.—Cf. *The Persecution of E. D. Morel*, Reformer's Series, Glasgow, 1919.

[30] The allusion is to Victor Hugo's *Les Burgraves*. Burgrave Job is eighty years of age; Burgrave Magnus, his son, is sixty.—Translators' Note.

[31] The section of Bellinzona, or of Ticino, was founded quite recently, in November, 1916. At the inaugural ceremony, the president, Julius Schmidhauser, delivered a speech in which he sounded an excellent European note. He contrasted the union of the three races of Switzerland with the spectacle of contemporary Europe still living in the prehistoric age, a Europe "wherein the Frenchman can see in the German nothing but an enemy, wherein the German can see in the Frenchman nothing but an enemy, and wherein neither can regard the other as a human being. For our part, we have a way in Switzerland of discovering the human element in all mankind."—"Centralblatt des Zofingervereins," December, 1916.

[32] The text was written in the summer of 1917. Shortly afterwards, fresh dissensions arose in the Zofingia. These discords have been accentuated by the Russian revolution.

[33] The program of the new committee (Der Centralausschuss an die Sektionen), published in the "Centralblatt" for October, 1916, was reproduced, in part, in the "Journal de Genève" for October 19th, under the caption Le programme de la Jeunesse. This program affirms the "supernationalist" and anti-imperialist faith on the lines expounded in the discussion of which a summary will shortly be given in the text. I quote from the program: "We do not live upon the worship of our warlike past.... Placed as we are in the centre of a system of great imperialist powers which aim at domination through force, at material greatness, and at glory, it is our task to fight openly, boldly, trusting in the future, against imperialism and on behalf of the ideal of humanity."

A keen interest in social questions, solidarity with the common people, with the disinherited of the earth, are likewise plainly manifested.

[34] None the less I am impressed by the bold and perspicuous idealism displayed by some of these young Latin Swiss in the discussions summarised in the sequel.

[35] Serment du Jeu de Paume, Versailles, June 20, 1789.—Translators' Note.

[36] Le Feu, Journal d'une Escouade, par Henri Barbusse, Flammarion, Paris, 1916. English translation, Under Fire, The Story of a Squad, Dent, London, 1917.

[37] Words of Farewell (issue of May, 1917).

[38] Among these I may mention my article, To the Murdered Nations (Chapter III, above) from which the censorship deleted one hundred lines. The gaps were filled by Wullens with Belot's fine engravings (issue of May, 1917).

[39] Notwithstanding the sentence passed upon Guilbeaux since the passage in the text was written, my confidence in him is unshaken. I differ from him in many respects, but I admire his courage. To those who have known Guilbeaux intimately, his good faith is above suspicion.—R. R., August, 1919.

[40] G. Thuriot-Franchi, Les Marches de France.

[41] Andreas Latzko, *Menschen im Krieg*, Rascher, Zurich, 1917; English translation, *Men in Battle*, Cassell, London, 1918.

[42] Andreas Latzko is a Hungarian officer. He was wounded on the Italian front during the fighting of 1915-16.

[43] Stefan Zweig, *Jeremias, eine dramatische Dichtung in neun Bildern*, Insel-Verlag, Leipzig, 1917.

[44] *Les Temps maudits*, "demain," Geneva.

[45] *Vous êtes des hommes*, "Nouvelle Revue Française," Paris; and *Poème contre le grand crime*, "demain," Geneva; above all the admirable *Danse des Morts*, "Les Tablettes," Geneva, republished by "L'Action Sociale," La-Chaux-de-Fonds.

[46] *Mr. Britling sees it Through*, Cassell, London, 1916.

[47] *The Fortune, a Romance of Friendship*, Maunsel, Dublin and London, 1917.

[48] G. F. Nicolai, M.D., sometime professor of physiology at Berlin University, *Die Biologie des Krieges, Betrachtungen eines Naturforschers den Deutschen zur Besinnung*, Orell Füssli, Zurich, 1917; English translation, *The Biology of War*, Dent, London, 1919.

[49] Cf. especially Chapter Six, an interesting account of the development of armies from ancient times down to to-day, when we have the armed nation. Also Chapter Fourteen, which deals with war and peace as reflected in the writings of ancient and modern poets and philosophers.

[50] Erfassen. Nicolai points out that the figurative meaning of the word "erfassen" like that of "apprehend" and "comprehend" [or of the native "grasp"] is a metaphysical extension of the primitive "prehension" by the hand.

[51] I ignore, in the text, the abundant proofs Nicolai draws from ethnology and from the history of the lower animals. He shows, for example, that the most primitive peoples, the Bushmen, the Fuegians, the Eskimos, etc., live in hordes even when they display no tendency towards family life. All savages are gregarious in the extreme; solitude is disastrous to them alike physically and mentally. Even civilised man finds solitude hard to bear.

[52] *Faust*, Part II, 5. Mephistopheles' words, when he hands over to Faust the proceeds of a voyage. [War, trade, and piracy are trinity in unity—inseparable.]

[53] "Everything which exists, above all everything which lives, tends towards immeasurable increase."

[54] For unicellular organisms, osmosis imposes a limit; for multicellular organisms there is a mechanical limit to size; for the groupings of individuals to form collectivities, social communities, there is a limit fixed by the amount of available energy.

[55] Pp. 160 to 163 [English edition].

[56] On p. 255 [of the English edition] will be found an ethnographical chart of Germany. It is distinctly humorous.

[57] This statement requires qualification. The reader is referred to a note at the end of the volume.

[58] Jeheber, Geneva, 1915.

[59] Buddhist Views of War, "The Open Court," May, 1904.

[60] The actual words in my play are: "The nations die that God may live."

[61] Nicolai terms them "chance products" (sind nur zufällige Produkte).

[62] It is surprising that there is but one mention of Auguste Comte in Nicolai's book; for Comte's Great Human Being is certainly akin to the German biologist's Humanity.

[63] We shall do well to note that Nicolai practically considers himself exempt from the need for these material demonstrations. As far as he is concerned, it would suffice him, as it sufficed Aristotle, to observe the play of forces among men. This simple observation would convince him that humanity must be regarded as an organism. "But moderns, although they will generally deny it, are for the most part infected with the belief that all solid fact must be material.... Even though it be not absolutely necessary to demonstrate that there exists between human beings a bridge of real substance (eine Brücke realer Substanz), even though the dynamic ties suffice us, it is desirable to satisfy the materialistic demands of our day, and to show that there does actually exist between the men of all ages and all lands an effective interconnection, which is uniform, persistent, nay eternal" [pp. 392-393, English edition].

[64] According to this theory, which was initiated by Gustav Jaeger in 1878, there occurs an eternal transmission of an inheritable germ plasm, this being temporarily housed within the perishable soma of

the individual living being. The hypothesis of the undying plasma has given rise to lively discussions which are still in progress.

[65] Ueber Ursprung und Bedeutung der Amphimixis, "Biolog. Zentralblatt," xxvi, No. 22, 1906.

[66] This seems to me the weak point in the theory. How can we reconcile the mutation and the variability of the germ plasm, with its immortality and its eternal transmission?

[67] Species and Varieties: their Origin by Mutation, Kegan Paul, London, 1905.

[68] Closing sections of Chapter Thirteen.

[69] I should like to give an account here of Nicolai's solution of the problem of liberty. He discusses the matter in one of the most important sections of his book.—How can a biologist, filled with a feeling of universal necessity, find place, amid that necessity and without prejudice to it, for human freedom? One of the most notable characteristics of this great mind, is Nicolai's power of associating within himself two rival and complementary forces. He makes a suggestive study, at once philosophic and physiological, of the anatomy of the brain and of the almost infinite possibilities the brain holds for the future (all unknown to us to-day), of the thousands of roads which are marked out in the brain many centuries before humanity dreams of using them.—But to follow up this study would lead us beyond the scope of the present article. I must refer the reader to pp. 58-68 of *The Biology of War* [English edition]. These pages are a model of scientific intuition.

[70] Chapter Ten, p. 309 [English edition].

[71] Chapter Fourteen.

[72] Chapter Ten, pp. 270-271 [English edition].

[73] Introduction, p. 11 [English edition].

[74] "Um dem guten und gerechten Menschen meine triumphierende Sicherheit zu geben." Introduction [p. 10, English edition].

[75] The most important of these studies have been collected in the great work *Les Fourmis de la Suisse* (Nouveaux mémoires de la Société helvétique des Sciences naturelles, vol. xxvi, Zurich, 1874), and in the admirable series *Expériences et remarques pratiques sur les sensations des insectes*, published in five parts in the "Rivista di Scienze biologiche," Como, 1900-1901. [Two only of Forel's writings on insects are available in the English language: *The Senses of Insects*, Methuen, London, 1908; and *Ants and some other Insects*, Kegan Paul, London, 1904.] But these works form no more than a fraction of the author's studies written on this subject. Dr. Forel recently told me that since the publication in 1874 of the work which has become a classic, he has penned no less than 226 essays upon ants.

[76] Some of these soldier ants function also as butchers, cutting up the prey into small fragments.

[77] *Insect Life*, Macmillan, London, 1901.

[78] *Mutual Aid*, Heinemann, London, 1915.

[79] Auguste Forel, *Les Fourmis de la Suisse*, pp. 261-263.

[80] Op. cit. p. 249.

[81] Polyergus rufescens.

[82] Op. cit. pp. 266-273.

[83] A great cause of error, among those who study insects, is to apply uncritically to an entire genus, observations made upon one or upon a few species. The species of insects are very numerous. Among ants alone, so Forel informs me, there are more than 7,500 species. These species exhibit all shades, all degrees, of instinct.

[84] I am well aware that the concluding statement in the text is in total contradiction with the thought of Auguste Forel, who denies free will. I do not propose here to reopen the agelong dispute between free will and determinism, which seems to me largely verbal. I shall consider the question elsewhere.

[85] For instance, the Institut für Kulturforschung (Institute for the Study of Civilisation) of Vienna (see above p. 19). This Institute has

just founded a Society for the Study of World Civilisation, which issues a periodical entitled "Erde, a journal for the intellectual life of the whole of mankind." The first number, which comes to hand while I am correcting the proof of these pages, is throughout an ardent confession of "panhumanist" faith.

[86] A Great European, G. F. Nicolai ("demain," October and November 1917).—See Chapter XX above.

[87] Steen Hasselbach, Copenhagen. First issue, October 1, 1918.

[88] Why I left Germany. An open letter to the Unknown who rules Germany.—The German article has been republished in pamphlet form by A. G. Benteli, Bümpliz-Bern, Switzerland, 1918.

[89] In telling this part of the story, Nicolai conceals most of the details of his flight. Too many are implicated, and they would suffer if he were explicit. Already, he tells us, an innocent person, the betrothed of one of his companions, has been imprisoned.—Some day he will write a memoir of his military experiences.

[90] This Aufruf an die Europäer is reprinted, in the first issue of "Das werdende Europa" immediately after the article I have just been analysing, and Nicolai appeals to all readers who sympathise with it to send him their signatures.

[91] Subsequent events have shown that this did not amount to much, after all. The moral abdication of President Wilson, abandoning his own principles without having the honesty to admit the fact, signalises the ruin of that lofty bourgeois idealism which, for a century and a half, gave to the ruling class, notwithstanding many mistakes, both strength and prestige. The consequences of such an act are incalculable.

Lightning Source UK Ltd.
Milton Keynes UK
UKHW040743160223
417123UK00001B/49

9 781006 933028